YAMIN NORAIM

A HIGH HOLIDAY COMPANION

YAMIM NORAIM

A High Holiday Companion

EDITED BY JONATHAN WITTENBERG

MASORTI PUBLICATIONS
LONDON 1996

First published in Great Britain
in 1995 by Masorti Publications

This second edition reset and
reprinted 1996

The Assembly of Masorti Synagogues
works for reasonableness and
responsiblity within tradition.

ISBN 0 9518002 2 1

Contents

Contributors

Rabbi Dr Louis Jacobs is Rabbi of the New London Synagogue.

Rabbi Chaim Weiner is Rabbi of Edgware Masorti Synagogue.

Rabbi Jonathan Wittenberg is Rabbi of the New North London Synagogue.

Ronnie Cohen is Ba'al Tefillah and Ba'al Tekiah at the New North London Synagogue.

Harry Freedman is Director of the Masorti Academy.

John Schlapobersky is a psychotherapist and author

Alex Sklan is Director of Social Services at Jewish Care.

לזכר נשמת

מרת מעשא בת ר" יעקב מאיר הלוי ע'ה
שהלכה לעולמה א טבת תשנ"ה

Dedicated in loving memory of

MERCIA ROSEN

28th March 1921 – 4th December 1994

Thus says the Lord:
'Restrain your voice from weeping,
your eyes from tears;
your work shall have its reward,'
says the Lord.

JEREMIAH 31: 15

כה אמר יהוה מנעי קולך מבכי ועיניך
מדמעה כי יש שכר לפעלתך נאם-יהוה

Introduction

The High Holidays are challenging, not to say overwhelming.

On the one hand they call us home. The well known melodies, the family memories, the full synagogue, the sound of the Shofar, these things mark the turn of the year and call us home to ourselves and to our God.

On the other hand the High Holidays present us with rich and complex laws and customs, a lengthy and often difficult liturgy and ideas which question the way we understand and live our lives. What does it mean to be judged by God? What are our responsibilities and how can we meet them? What do we want to uphold in our lives and what do we need to change?

This book is intended to be just what its title says, a companion to help the person looking for guidance and explanation through the High Holiday period. It makes no attempt to be exhaustive. But in examining our most important practices and prayers it provides a close and often personal focus on the essential themes of the season.

The book is divided into three sections. The first is a study of key laws and customs, such as the blowing of the Shofar, the giving of charity, repentance and fasting. On each topic a page of traditional sources from the Bible and rabbinic writings has been placed side by side with a page of contemporary commentary. In this way Jewish teachings are directly related to how we can try to understand them and honour them in our own lives.

The second part is a guide to twelve essential prayers. They have been chosen not only for their liturgical importance, but also because each one offers the opportunity to concentrate on a different theme or issue. In every case a double page is devoted first to a short history and explanation of the prayer, and then to one or more interpretations suggesting what it may mean in the context of our concerns today.

The last part of the book is a series of reflections which follow the progress of the High Holiday season and its drama from before Rosh Hashanah until the beginning of Succot. It addresses some of the emotional and spiritual dilemmas with which we are inevitably confronted.

The core of this book consists of the writings of the rabbis of the Masorti Movement in Great Britain. It is supplemented by a rich range of wider contributions, all acknowledged in their place, so as to stimulate thought and convey the understanding that there are many ways of approaching our prayers and beliefs.

The book can be used as a reference, read in sections or in its entirety. We hope it will prove a fertile source of reflections and help to make the liturgy and traditions of the High Holidays more accessible to us and us more amenable to them.

JONATHAN WITTENBERG

הלכות והליכות

Laws and Customs

Elul

SOURCES

The Lord is my light and my salvation, who shall I fear? The Lord is the strength of my life of whom shall I be afraid? . . . PSALM 2

The Sages explain this with reference to the High Holidays:

My light – this is Rosh Hashanah; My salvation – this is Yom Kippur MIDRASH TEHILLIM 27

For He will hide me in His tabernacle in the time of trouble, in the secret of His tent He will conceal me . . . PSALM 27

This clearly refers to Succot.

There is a tradition that the world was created on Rosh Hashanah. The first thing to be created was light. Therefore the opening line of Psalm 27 puts us in mind both of Rosh Hashanah and Yom Kippur. Later in the Psalm we find the word Succah. Hence the custom developed of reading Psalm 27 throughout the High Holiday period.

On the first day of Elul the Holy One, blessed be He, said to Moses: 'Come up the mountain to me.' They blew the Shofar in the camp when Moses was ascending the mountain, in order that they should no longer commit the sin of idolatry . . . Therefore the Sages ordained that the Shofar should be blown each year on the first day of Elul. PIRKEI D'RABBI ELIEZER 46

According to tradition it was on Yom Kippur that God forgave the Israelites for the sin of the golden calf. This followed Moses' ascent of Mount Sinai for the second time, where he spent forty days prostrated in prayer and fasting (Deuteronomy 9: 18–29). The first of Elul is forty days before Yom Kippur, hence it is assumed that this is the day on which Moses ascended the mountain.

COMMENT

Elul, the month before New Year, marks the beginning of the period leading up to the Days of Awe. The majesty and splendour of the High Holidays, and the trepidation and drama which they evoke, are so powerful that we cannot simply arrive at Rosh Hashanah unprepared. Elul allows us time to acclimatise, to consider how we are going to approach the High Holidays and how we are going to respond to the spiritual demands that they place upon us. It allows us to review our relationships with those around us, to repair any wounds and to strengthen our commitments to each other and to God.

We blow the Shofar each morning in the synagogue as a reminder of the solemnity of the season and of the tasks ahead of us.

Immediately after the blowing of the Shofar we recite Psalm 27. The manner in which the Midrash links it to the High Holiday period hints at a deeper idea, that the sentiments contained in this Psalm go to the heart of the meaning of the season.

Psalm 27 expresses our trust and faith in God: 'Wait for the Lord, be strong and encourage your heart, and wait for the Lord.' It articulates the hope that we can develop spiritually, so that we will be able to rise above our worldly cares and problems: 'One thing I have asked of the Lord, this I will request, that I may dwell in the House of the Lord all the days of my life.' Above all else, Elul is the period at which we try to renew our relationship with God. Psalm 27 is a sublime expression of this wish.

HARRY FREEDMAN

Selichot

SOURCES

It is customary to rise towards dawn and to say prayers of forgiveness and supplication from the beginning of Elul onwards. The custom of the Ashkenazi communities is not so, but rather from the beginning of Elul the Shofar is blown every day after the morning service . . . and they rise towards dawn to recite Selichot from the Sunday preceding Rosh Hashanah, and if Rosh Hashanah falls on a Monday or a Tuesday, then they start from the Sunday before that.

SHUKHAN ARUCH, ORACH HAYYIM 581

Rabbi Eliezer says: The night has three watches, and at each watch the Holy One, blessed be He, sits and roars like a lion. For it is written: The Lord does roar from on high, and raise His voice from His holy habitation; 'roaring He doth roar' because of His fold. (Jeremiah 25: 30)

TALMUD BERACHOT 2B

From here we learn that the time of the changing of the watches is particularly appropriate for prayer

Lord, You have taught us to recite the thirteen,
Remember unto us today the covenant of the thirteen
As You revealed it to the meek one in days past.
As it is written: And the Lord descended in a cloud and stood with him there,
And he called out in the name of the Lord. (Exodus 34: 5)

FROM THE SELICHOT SERVICE

At the end of the day of rest we have come before You.
Lend an ear, Exalted, who sits in glory,
To hear our prayer and our supplication.

Receive their supplication as they rise at night,
Accept it as a whole offering unto You.
Reveal unto them your miracles, God who does great deeds.

HYMN FOR THE FIRST NIGHT OF SELICHOT

סליחות

COMMENT

It is a fact of life that few things of value happen by themselves. Events that are meaningful take a lot of preparation before they happen. Frequently the preparation for the event is as important as the event itself. This is true even in the realm of religious living. It is for this reason that the High Holiday period does not just 'drop' upon us. The tradition provides for a warming up period during the month leading up to Rosh Hashanah. The exact extent of this period depends on local custom.

The Selichot service takes place in the early morning hours during the lead up period to Rosh Hashanah and Yom Kippur. It has a special atmosphere which is created by the early morning hours. The mystics were well aware of a special quality to stillness of night, and understood that it its a time when God is specially tuned into our prayers. The liturgy of the Selichot service has overtones of the High Holiday liturgy. It is the first time that the special melodies and the modes of the High Holidays are heard, and this fact by itself draws many to the synagogues to the Selichot service. The service consists of a series of special piyyutim, or hymns, around the theme of repentance or forgiveness. The choice of hymns differs from community to community, but the central element of the service is always the recitation of God's thirteen attributes as they appear in Exodus 34: 6–7:

The Lord, the Lord God, merciful and gracious, long suffering, and abundant in goodness and truth, keeping mercy for thousands, forgiving iniquity and transgression and sin, and who surely forgives.

The reason that these verses are recited goes back to the story of the golden calf, in the book of Exodus. This is the context from which they are taken. After Moses prays for forgiveness for the people and the people have repented for their sin, Moses asks God to 'see His honour'. Since it is inconceivable that Moses would be asking to see God Himself, the Rabbis understand that he is actually asking God for the secret to God's forgiveness. According to this tradition, God wraps Himself up in a tallit and tephillin, and recites these thirteen attributes, saying: In the future, when you need forgiveness, this is what you should say.

There are many different ways that we stand before God over the High Holiday season. Sometimes we beg or beseech. At other times, we recite prayers that remind God of His promises, or of the merit of our ancestors. Some of our prayers detail our suffering for the sake of our beliefs. This prayer suggests that we will be forgiven because, at an early time in our history, God let us in on a special secret. The Selichot service combines all of these sentiments together in preparation for the High Holidays.

CHAIM WEINER

Repentance

SOURCES

Return, O Israel, unto the Lord your God; for you have stumbled in your iniquity. Take with you words, and return to the Lord. Say unto him: 'Forgive all iniquity and accept that which is good.

HOSEA 14: 2–3

Of what does repentance consist? That the sinner abandon their sin, remove it from their thought and resolve in their heart not to do it again, as it is said: 'Let the wicked forsake their way.' One should regret the fact that one transgressed, as it is said: 'For after I had returned I was sorry.' One should make God who knows all hidden things one's witness that one will never again return to this sin, as it is said: 'We will no more say "our gods" of the works of our hands.' One must confess verbally, stating those matters which one has resolved in one's heart. MAIMONIDES: LAWS OF REPENTANCE 2: 2

Rabbi Zusya of Hanipol said: There are five verses in the Bible which constitute the essence of Judaism. They begin in Hebrew with one of these letters: 'Tav, Shin, Vav, Beth, Heh', which comprise the Hebrew word for Repentance: 'Teshuvah'.

Tav: You shall be wholehearted with the Lord your God.
DEUTERONOMY 18: 13
Shin: I keep the Lord before me always. PSALM 16: 8
Vav: You shall love your neighbour as you love yourself.
LEVITICUS 19: 18
Beth: In all your ways acknowledge Him. PROVERBS 3: 6
Heh: To walk humbly with your God. MICAH 6: 8

Therefore, resolve to act accordingly so that your repentance may be sincere. HASSIDIC

With everlasting kindness will I have compassion on you, says the Lord, your Redeemer . . . For the mountains may depart, and the hills be removed; but My kindness shall not depart from you, neither shall My covenant of peace be removed, says the Lord who has compassion on you. ISAIAH 54: 8–10

COMMENT

It has been said that God sets out towards us on Rosh Hashanah and, ten days later on Yom Kippur, we are free to set out towards God. The word teshuvah means return, denoting completion and recommencement in a cycle that holds out the promise of change as we come back to our origins. When we ask ourselves, 'Who am I? What have I done? Where will next year find me?', the past and the future – memory and hope – come together, allowing us to focus on our character and make-up, giving new significance to the whole of our lives. With the birth of the New Year, life ahead of us is rich in the prospect of new beginnings. And, to prepare for it, we undergo a ritual of purification on Yom Kippur that confirms our freedom to make our own choices. In the 'still, small voice' there is not only the note of judgement but that of transformation, a note by which we are called to work on the business of change. Through the services we remind ourselves and one another that teshuvah, prayer and charity can alter the destiny of our fate.

Teshuvah is a broader term than penitence which is its most common translation, and describes the restoration of spiritual vitality. This is a dual experience of both acquittal that involves forgiveness, and atonement that leads to purification. From the opening mood of the penitential prayers preceding Rosh Hashanah, to the intense, imploring quality of Neilah at the close of Yom Kippur, there is a progression that begins with regret and concludes with redemption. Based on the teaching of our rabbis, the liturgy invites us to find words for the evident as well as for the unseen afflictions in the heartland of the self. Whenever we face the challenge of our freedom in the knowledge of good and evil, we struggle with painful choices. Finding words for what is wrong gives us new opportunities to put it right. The emotions of regret that open the cycle of this season can sharpen to remorse as we examine ourselves. And, if we are sincere in this struggle, it can lead us to private and personal acts of reparation through which to make good, redeeming our lost sense of innocence and allowing us – through prayer – to once again come close to the sacred.

We begin the festivals with a mood of regret in the penitential prayers. They lead us to prepare for and celebrate the Creation on Rosh Hashanah with a sense of awe. Ten days later we begin Kol Nidrei as a self-constituted assembly in law seeking and granting authority to pray in the presence of sinners. Everyone is capable of repenting; all are qualified to stand before God and renew our covenant with him. The Children of Israel, standing together in the most near and far-flung places of the world, mark in our congregations a sacred time and place in which to seek God's presence and renewal.

JOHN SCHLAPOBERSY

Prayer

SOURCES

I shall sing to the Lord with my life, make music for my God as long as I have being.

PSALM 104: 33

Out of the depths have I called upon You, O Lord. Lord, listen to my voice.

PSALM 130: 1–2

One should not rise to pray in a state of sadness, nor in a state of idleness, nor amidst laughter, casual conversation or levity of mind, nor out of idle occupations, but in a spirit of joy in the performance of the commandments.

TALMUD BERACHOT 31A

When one prays one should focus one's mind on the meaning of the words one is saying. One should think to oneself as if the Shechinah is before one. One should so far remove all preoccupations from the mind that one's thought and concentration remain pure throughout one's prayer . . . One should think on matters which humble the heart, focusing it on our Father in heaven.

SHUKHAN ARUCH: ORACH HAYYIM 98: 1

Say your prayers in a melody that is most pleasant and sweet to you. Then you shall pray with proper kavvanah (intention), because the melody will draw your heart after the words that come from your mouth. Supplicate in a melody that makes the heart weep, praise in a melody that makes the heart glad.

SEFER HASIDIM: 11

Those who run precipitately through the liturgy, rushing in and out of the prayer texts, as if the task were to cover a maximum of space in a minimum of time, will derive little from worship. To be able to pray is to know how to stand still and to dwell upon a word . . . There is a classical principle in regard to prayer 'Better is a little with kavvanah (direction of the heart) than much without it' (Tur, Orach Hayim 61).

A J HESCHEL: *QUEST FOR GOD,* p. 34–5

תפלה

COMMENT

Prayer, like charity and repentance, is one of the three things which have, according to our tradition, the power to change our lives. Over the High Holidays we spend many hours attending prayers, traversing hundreds of pages of liturgy and saying God's name thousands of times. Yet to pray truly is something which most of us find very difficult indeed. For prayer has its roots in the heart. We may share the communal setting and a common form of worship, but ultimately the meaning of our prayers depends on the sincerity of our personal involvement in them.

What, then, can help us, and what may hinder us, in our desire to pray?

It can help us to feel that in our prayers we have the support of those around us who are trying to achieve the same thing, that our private searching is strengthened by the collective endeavour of the whole congregation. It helps us to be aware that we pray within the context of a great spiritual tradition and that those who have gone before us have fashioned and sanctified a pathway that leads to God, and are with us as we travel along the same road.

It is reassuring to know that we do not always have to keep up with every line of our extensive liturgy. On the contrary, we must also give ourselves time to pause and reflect. Indeed, the beautiful words and stirring melodies are also there to help us find ourselves. Through them God reaches out to us, so that we can reach out to God. This does not happen easily or in a rush. We should be realistic; hours in Synagogue may include only a few minutes of real devotion. But a few minutes can be a lot.

It hinders us to have expectations of prayer. Too often prayer is understood exclusively as the desire to change God's mind 'God, please do this!', 'God, please don't do that!' we say. After all, each of us wants health, peace and wellbeing for the people we love, and for everyone. But the danger is that if our wishes are frustrated we will feel that God doesn't listen; when our hopes are disappointed we will conclude that there is no God.

Prayer, however, is more than a list of requests, more even than thanksgiving and confession. In prayer we set our life in the context of a greater reality. There we may find ourselves not so much asking as being asked of. The voice of fine silence may be followed by a question, as it was for Elijah on the mountain of the Lord: 'What are you doing here?' Truly to seek God is to be challenged, as well as to be blessed.

JONATHAN WITTENBERG

Charity

SOURCES

Righteousness, righteousness shall you pursue.

DEUTERONOMY 16: 20

The giving of charity is equal to all the other commandments combined.

TALMUD BAVA BATRA 9B

Rabbi Elazar said: The reward of giving charity depends entirely on the measure of kindness with which it is done.

TALMUD SUKKAH 49B

There are eight degrees of charity, one higher than the other. The highest degree of charity exceeded by none is that of the person who assists a poor Jew by providing him with a gift or loan or by accepting him into a business partnership or by helping him find employment – in a word, by putting him in a situation where he can dispense with other people's aid.

Below this is the person who gives to charity in such a way that he does not know to whom he is giving and the recipient does not know from whom he is taking. For this shows that the commandment is being performed for its own sake. [Within this category] is the person who puts money into the charity box.

MAIMONIDES: LAWS OF GIFTS TO THE NEEDY 10: 7–8

COMMENT

Giving charity is central to the Jewish way of life. It teaches us to care for our fellow human beings and gives us a sense of purpose.

Judaism is, however, realistic about human nature and, as always, turns the mission statement into a practical plan of action. Thus 'righteousness, righteousness shall you pursue' becomes a command to give regularly a proportion of what we have. Maimonides rules that to give up to a fifth of one's income is to fulfil the commandment perfectly, that to give a tenth is average but that to provide less is considered stingy (Gifts to the Needy 8: 8). Nevertheless, Judaism knows at one extreme of saintly individuals who have given everything, while at the other it encourages even the poorest of the poor to try to give something.

Of course, it is best to give from the heart, but those in need cannot wait for the right mood to come over us. Tzedakah is therefore understood more as a form of self taxation than as a donation to be given only when we feel like it. Indeed the very word 'tzedakah' implies doing that which is 'right', that which we are duty bound to do.

To whom should we give and how should we do so? Our responsibilities are for our own immediate family first, for those in our own communities next, for our people and then for humankind. These priorities should influence how we apportion our charitable giving. In the first place we should give to people in need within our community, then to people who are in need of the help of Jewish welfare charities because local communities do not have the resources to assist them. Next come our fellow Jews in Eastern Europe and in Israel and then all people in need throughout the world: fellow human beings who are starving, oppressed or homeless. We have constant responsibilities to all these groups.

How we give is important. The best way is to give people the means to live as independently as they are able. That can be achieved through the provision of employment, independent living accommodation, means of transport or access to facilities. This may apply equally to carers themselves, imprisoned by their obligation to look after someone close to them entirely on their own. They too need the means to carry out their obligations – relief and support on both the emotional and practical levels.

We should give anonymously but satisfy ourselves that if help is given through a charity it is delivered in a way that preserves the independence, dignity and self respect of the recipient.

Throughout the liturgy on the High Holidays we chant: 'Repentance, prayer and charity will avert the harshness of the decree.' To paraphrase Abraham Joshua Heschel, maybe all these efforts will not save us, but at least they will make us worth saving.

ALEX SKLAN

The Shofar

SOURCES

And in the seventh month, on the first day of the month, you shall have a holy convocation; you shall do no manner of servile work; it is a day of blowing the horn unto you.

BEMIDBAR 29: 1

God is gone up amidst shouting, the Lord amidst the sound of the Shofar

PSALM 47: 6

Rabbi Abbahu said: Why does one blow a Shofar [made from] a ram? The Holy One, blessed be He, said: Blow before Me a Shofar made from a ram, so that I remember unto you the binding of Isaac, son of Abraham, and account it unto you as if you had bound yourselves before Me.

TALMUD ROSH HASHANAH 16A

The Shofar which is sounded both on Rosh Hashanah and for the Jubilee is a bent ram's horn. All Shofarot other than that of a ram's horn are unacceptable.

MAIMONIDES: HILCHOT SHOFAR 1: 1

The great Shofar shall be sounded and the voice of fine silence will be heard

THE UNETANNEH TOKEF PRAYER

Happy are the people who know the sound of the Teruah. O Lord, they will walk in the light of Your countenance.

PSALM 89: 16

COMMENT

The only Mitzvah which the Torah commands us to perform on Rosh Hashanah other than the offering of sacrifices is the blowing of the Shofar. But despite this, the Torah does not give us any details regarding the kind of Shofar or the number and type of notes to be blown. However, the Rabbis noted that the word Teruah is mentioned in the Torah three times in connection with the blowing of the Shofar and, according to tradition, each Teruah is preceded and followed by a single long blast known as a Tekiah. Thus, the minimum number of notes which a person is obligated to hear is nine (three Teruot and six Tekiot) although this number has been substantially increased so that in Ashkenazi synagogues, it is now customary to blow 100 notes on each of the two days of Rosh Hashanah unless the first day falls on Shabbat, in which case the Shofar is not sounded at all on that day.

The essential element of the Mitzvah is the Teruah since this is the only note specifically mentioned in the Torah. But over the passage of years and during the numerous exiles, doubts were raised concerning the Teruah to the extent that the exact sound was not known, although it is possible that from a very early stage there was more than one practice concerning the Teruah. Some maintained that it should be a 'wailing' tone such as 'women utter when they lament'. Others maintained that it should resemble a 'sigh' which a person might repeatedly utter in a state of acute anxiety. Or possibly it should be a combination of the two! To accommodate both views, the 'sigh' was called Shevarim and was identified by three broken notes, whilst the 'wailing' was called Teruah and consisted of a series of short staccato notes.

It is true to say that the blowing of the Shofar has become the central part of the Rosh Hashanah service. We are all familiar with that very special moment when the Baal Tekiah raises the Shofar to his lips. There is no more dramatic moment in the entire liturgy. The whole congregation waits with bated breath, tense and expectant. When the first Tekiah is blown, the raw primeval sound echoes through the silent synagogue. Individually, we are transported back to the time when we stood as children and marvelled at the blowing of the Shofar. Collectively, the whole congregation is fused for an instant into one body supporting the Baal Tekiah, willing him to blow with strength and stamina and hoping against hope that he will not run into difficulties.

The sound which rises from the Shofar to God is the same sound as was heard on Mount Sinai at the giving of the Torah and reminds us of our beginnings as a people. The Shofar forms a link with our people's long distant past and our own immediate past. But it also carries us forward into the future, bearing our hopes and our dreams.

RONNIE COHEN

Making Peace with One's Fellow

SOURCES

A gentle response turns anger aside.

PROVERBS 15: 1

Yom Kippur makes atonement for transgressions between a person and God. Yom Kippur does not make atonement for transgressions between one person and another until pardon has been procured.

MISHNAH YOMA 8: 9

Transgressions between one person and another, such as if a person injured another, or cursed another, or robbed another and so forth, are never forgiven until one has restored to one's fellow what is due and pardon has been obtained. Even if the money due has been returned, one must seek pardon and ask for forgiveness. Even if it is only through something one said that one has upset one's fellow, one must apologise, entreating until one has obtained forgiveness.

It is forbidden a person to be cruel and to refuse to accept an apology. Rather, one should forgive readily and be hard to anger, so that when a wrongdoer comes to ask pardon one grants it willingly and with one's whole heart.

MAIMONIDES: LAWS OF REPENTANCE 2: 9–10

Rava said: All the sins are overlooked of those who overlook offences against themselves.

TALMUD YOMA 87B

COMMENT

We are charged at this season with the challenge of finding peace in our personal relations. The High Holidays are a time for reconciliation, whether this is to be found in a positive act of restitution, or in the generosity of spirit with which we receive another person's apologies. But when we consider the wrongs that lie between people, the questions are so complex and difficult, they touch the roots of both ethics and psychology and embrace all our social bonds.

These matters present themselves to us with a new urgency at this time – political wrongs in the abuse of power; economic wrongs in the maldistribution of resources; the wrongs of war, personal violence, the emotional neglect of a friend or relative, or an act of dishonesty, deceit or cruelty. Who is guilty and of what? What does restitution mean? When you look in the injured eyes of someone betrayed by their parents, partner or society, what does restitution require? Making good may be a life time's endeavour, rather than the gesture of a moment. Is our culpability measured by the consequences of our actions or by the nature of our intentions? And who does the measuring?

When we 'pour out our souls' in the confessional prayers, what is it we declare ourselves guilty of? Our relations with others can be understood in terms of both individual and collective responsibility. Firstly, the 'transgressions between one person and another' – those that arise in personal relations of any kind – require that we make good, person to person. Only when others let go of what they hold against us can we be released. Only when we release others from the burden of our own enmity or hatred, can we draw back to make peace with ourselves, let the grievance go and move forward in freedom. Beyond this there is no simple formula for the discharge of a personal wrong. We have all known what it is to live with the burdens of anger and blame. Each of us has struggled with guilt and remorse and has had to work hard to find acceptable ways of making good. We have all enjoyed the relief of doing so. Guilt and shame are the marks of our humanity, the emotions by which we are connected with those who suffer on our account. Resolving these emotions can release us from the invisible ties that otherwise bind us to our regrets.

Secondly, at the collective level, there is a strange paradox to this season. We are each alone as we review our personal conduct and at the same time we are all together as we assume a collective responsibility for the behaviour of all. We stand alone, we stand together and we stand responsible, in part at least, for all that transpires around us.

JOHN SCHLAPOBERSKY

Fasting

SOURCES

Also on the tenth day of this seventh month there shall be a day of atonement; it shall be a holy gathering to you; and you shall afflict your souls, and offer an offering made by fire to the Lord. And you shall do no work in that same day; for it is a day of atonement, to make an atonement for you before the Lord your God. For whatever soul it is who shall not be afflicted in that same day, he shall be cut off from among his people.

LEVITICUS 23: 27–9

On the day of atonement it is forbidden to eat, to drink, to wash, to anoint oneself, to put on sandals, or to have marital relations.

MISHNAH YOMA 8: 1

What is the order [of service] for fast days? The ark is taken out to the open space of the city, wood ashes are placed upon the ark, on the head of the Nasi and on the head of the Ab-Beth-Din. Everyone else puts ashes on his own head; the elder among them addresses them with words of admonition [to repentance].

MISHNAH TA'ANIT 2: 1

Is not this rather the fast that I have chosen? To loose the chains of wickedness, to undo the bands of the yoke, and to let the oppressed go free, and to break every yoke? Is it not to share your bread with the hungry, and that you bring the poor, who are cast out, to your house? When you see the naked, that you cover him; and that you hide not yourself from your own flesh?

ISAIAH 58: 6–7

Mar Zutra says: The merit of a fast day lies in the charity dispensed.

TALMUD BERACHOT 6B

COMMENT

From very early times, prayers of petition have been accompanied with fasting. Instinctively people have felt that to pray alone is not enough. Fasting made the prayers say more. The messages that fasting naturally suggests to us are many. On a basic level, it allows us to feel that we are not asking for something for free. We are also willing to give of ourselves, and there is nothing more fundamental that we can give than what we see as our basic right to eat and drink. On a deeper level, it is a reminder of how dependent we are on God's gifts, that even for our most basic needs we are always no more than one step away from the grave, and that even if deprived of them for a short time our lives become untenable.

On another level, fasting focuses our attention on ourselves. It reminds us of our vulnerability. By appearing small before God, by being vulnerable, we hope to arouse his compassion. We wish to remind him that we are but flesh and blood, and remain forever in his hands. Thus we hope that he will take our smallness into account, and disregard our transgressions much as a parent is constantly making allowances for her child.

However, as effective a tool as fasting is in enhancing prayer, there are also inherent risks as there are risks in any religious activity. The real danger is seeing fasting as an end in itself, as something worth pursuing for its own sake. Fasting is a tool, an aid, just as prayer itself is only a means to achieve the 'real' religious aims. There is a danger that people will not move beyond this tool, will dedicate their lives to excessive fasting, to constant prayer, without taking its lessons and applying them to everyday life. There is the danger that, once we feel we have payed the price, God's forgiveness is seen as automatic, as deserved and acquired. The haftarah on Yom Kippur reminds us: it is not fasting that God requires, it is caring for the needy, feeding the hungry and clothing the poor. It is by emulating those qualities in God for which we beseech when we fast that ultimately we make ourselves worthy of God's blessings and forgiveness. If fasting does not lead to this, then it becomes no more than an empty exercise.

CHAIM WEINER

Confession

SOURCES

And Aaron shall lay both his hands upon the head of the live goat, and confess over him all the iniquities of the children of Israel, and all their transgressions, even all their sins; and he shall put them upon the head of the goat, and shall send him away by the hand of an appointed man into the wilderness. And the goat shall bear upon him all their iniquities into a land which is cut off; and he shall let go the goat in the wilderness.

LEVITICUS 16: 21–2

[The High Priest] would then come to the goat that was to be sent away, lay his two hands upon it and confess. This is what he would say: 'O God, Your people Israel have committed iniquity, transgressed, and sinned before You. I beseech You, by Your name, forgive the iniquities, transgressions and sins which Your people the House of Israel have committed and transgressed and sinned before You, as it is written in the Torah of Moses Your servant: For on this day shall atonement be made for you to cleanse you; from all your sins shall you be clean before the Lord' (Leviticus 16: 30). When the priests and the people standing in the Temple court heard the ineffable name as it came from the lips of the High Priest, they would kneel and prostrate themselves and fall on their faces, and say: 'Blessed be the Name, the glory of whose kingdom is for ever and ever.'

MISHNAH YOMA 6: 2

If a person transgresses any of the commands of the Torah, whether positive or negative, whether deliberately or by mistake, when he repents and returns from his sin he must confess before God, blessed be He, as it is written: 'Speak to the people of Israel: When a man or woman shall commit any sin . . . Then they shall confess their sin which they have done' (Numbers 5: 6–7). This is a verbal confession. This obligation of confession is a positive commandment. How does one confess? Say: 'Please, God, I have sinned, transgressed and committed an iniquity before you. I have done such and such a thing. I regret my action and am ashamed of what I have done. I will never repeat this thing again.' This is the essence of the confession. All who add to this are to be praised.

MAIMONIDES: THE LAWS OF REPENTANCE 1: 1

COMMENT

According to Maimonides, confession is an essential part of the act of repentance. It is not sufficient to just 'feel sorry' about the things that we have done in the past, or to decide to change our ways and behave differently in the future. It is not even enough to just 'think' a confession. The decision to change must be accompanied by a verbal statement which includes a 'recap' of the mistakes that one has made, and a positive commitment not to repeat those mistakes again in the future.

Why is this verbal confession necessary? Rabbi J. Soloveitchik suggests that this is because there is a big difference between the things that we think and the things that we say. There are always thoughts going around in our minds. Today we feel one thing and tomorrow we feel otherwise. Sometimes our thoughts are not focused. We think, but we haven't thought things through to the end, we aren't even aware that we have missed some of the angles.

When we speak, things are different. Consider when you are asked to speak in public. The act of putting your thoughts into words is very hard work. It helps to make your thoughts clear, even to yourself, sometimes for the first time. You must have a clearer picture of what it is you really want to say.

Furthermore, confession gives the act of repentance a definite time and place in our lives. Repentance doesn't just happen. It is a long process of self examination, of evaluation and decision making. It is hard to mark one point along this path which is the 'moment' that a person has changed. Confession marks out an actual point in time that the process of repentance has come to fruition. It is a moment in time to work towards, and a bench mark to look back upon and ask whether we have succeeded or failed to live up to our expectations from ourselves.

CHAIM WEINER

Atonement

SOURCES

For on this day shall atonement be made for you, to cleanse you; from all your sins before the Lord shall you be cleansed.

LEVITICUS 16: 30

Rabbi Akiva said: Happy are you, Israel! Before whom do you cleanse yourselves? Who cleanses you? Your Father in heaven! For it is said: 'I shall pour over you clean water and you shall be cleansed,' and it is said: 'The hope (Mikveh) of Israel is the Lord.' Just as the Mikveh cleanses the unclean, so does the Holy One, blessed be He, cleanse Israel.

MISHNAH YOMA 8: 9

For through our many sins we have stripped ourselves of the sacred divine image that clothed us . . . exchanging it for an impure image, putting on garments of filth . . . Have mercy on us and command Your holy angels responsible for matters of purity to remove the filthy garments from us. Cleanse us from all our sins and clothe us again in the garment of holiness . . . according to the prayer of King David, peace be upon him: Restore to me the joy of Your salvation; with a generous spirit support me. A pure heart create for us, God; put into us new spirit.

AVRAHAM DANZIG: TEFILLAH ZAKKAH

Who is a God like You, pardoning iniquity and passing over transgression for the remnant of his heritage? He does not hold onto His anger forever, for He delights in mercy. He will return, He will have compassion on us, He will overcome our iniquities. You will throw all their sins into the depths of the sea.

MICAH 7: 18–9

COMMENT

Yom Kippur may not hold the secret of perpetual youth, but it certainly opens the possibility of perpetual renewal. According to the Talmud (Niddah 30b) every child is taught the whole Torah before it leaves its mother's womb. When its studies are complete the child is told that the soul implanted within it is pure, and is adjured to preserve it in its purity. One does not have to take this story literally to appreciate that something essential is being communicated about human nature and potential. Everyday we remind ourselves of this when we pray: 'My God, the soul You gave me is pure, You created it, You fashioned it, You breathed it into me.'

However, it is virtually impossible to live for a single hour, let alone year, without losing touch with both purity, God and soul. It is of course a truism, but we are only human. Life challenges us in all sorts of ways and we say, plan and do things that we later regret. We are inextricably engaged in a cycle of action and reaction, responsibility and response. If there is a still point to our turning world, if we feel a sense of closeness to the one God, it is for most of us only rarely, and it eludes us almost as soon as it comes.

Once a year, therefore, we are given the opportunity to devote an entire day to returning home, to the rediscovery of closeness with God. 'Seek ye the Lord while He is to be found', declared the prophet Isaiah, and our rabbis understood this to refer to the period from Rosh Hashanah till Yom Kippur. 'Seek ye the Lord' teaches us that we have to make the effort: 'while He is to be found' indicates that God is waiting, even looking, for us to do so. It is as if together we have to take back down the barriers that have been built up between us over the year. We have been untrue to our ideals and unfaithful to our intuitions of the person we might have been. But it is not just us; the world has also been difficult, life painful. We have plenty to argue about with God. Therefore we need the day of Yom Kippur and the inner work of repentance. They have the power to turn distance back to closeness.

Jewish teaching is always realistic. There are, as we well know, harsh experiences which set their mark on an entire life. Equally, character traits, however much we may regret them, are scarcely ever entirely erased. We may suffer from both till the end of our days. But once a year our hope and our ideals are restored in the understanding of who we are and who we can be: at one with God.

JONATHAN WITTENBERG

תפלות

Prayers

Remember us for life, King who delights in life, and write us in the book of life for Your sake, living God

ZOCHRENU LECHAIM – REMEMBER US FOR LIFE

In each of our prayers throughout the ten days of penitence from Rosh Hashanah evening until Ne'ilah we make four short but significant additions.

In the first blessing of the Amidah we add: Remember us for life, King who delights in life, and write us in the book of life for Your sake, God of life.

In the second: Who is like You, merciful Father, in mercy remembering Your creatures for life.

In the penultimate: Inscribe all the children of Your covenant for a good life.

In the last: May we and all Your people the House of Israel be remembered and inscribed in the book of life and blessing, peace and prosperity, for a good life and for peace.

Probably it is the very simplicity of these prayers that have made them so popular Yet, in spite of their brevity, they introduce us to the key themes of this season, matters which will be explored in depth in other, more expansive passages. All four insertions refer to life: three of them employ the image of writing in the book of life. We do not know exactly who composed them. We learn of their existence from debates among the Geonim (the leaders of Babylonian Jewry from the seventh to the beginning of the eleventh centuries) as to whether it is fitting to include such requests as these in the opening blessings of the Amidah, normally devoted exclusively to the praise of God. The texts have come down to us from the Siddur of Rav Amram Gaon (ninth century) and have since been included in all the liturgical traditions

We ask God who loves life to write us in the book of life. This image has its roots in the Bible, where the prophet Malachi speaks of a book of remembrance being 'written before him for those who feared the Lord and took heed of his name'. The scholar Israel Abrahams suggests that the idea may have originated in the register or civil list drawn up in Judea in which the names of fully qualified citizens were entered. But whatever its origin it is a fearful picture, for we are taught that at this season 'the books of the living and the books of the dead are open before God' (Talmud: Arachin 10b). Rabbi Cruspedai said quoting Rabbi Yochanan: 'Three books are opened on Rosh Hashanah, one for the entirely wicked, one for the entirely righteous, and one for those between' (Talmud: Rosh Hashanah 16b). This is the source for the seasonal greeting: 'May you be inscribed for a good life.'

These phrases remind us sharply of our mortality. God will weigh us and judge us, and if God finds us wanting, so the idea suggests, our days will be curtailed. Yet God does not want to mete out such a measure. God delights in life, as it is said: 'I have no desire for anyone to die, says the Lord God; so return and live' (Ezekiel 18: 32). Thus life and death depend ultimately on us and on our conduct. It is we who by our deeds separate ourselves from God and life; the inscription in the

זכרנו לחיים, מלך חפץ בחיים, וכתבנו בספר החיים,
למענך אלהים חיים

book is written primarily by ourselves.

There is both comfort and anguish in this thought. The anguish is itself twofold. In the first place, can we and should we really believe that God takes away life as a form of punishment? In the second place, we are confronted with the inevitable reflection that the world and its fortunes do not confirm the idea that goodness is rewarded with length of days. On the contrary: suffering is to all appearances most unjustly distributed. In the end these prayers bring home to us the painful mystery of life and death and our ignorance of how, when and why we die.

The comfort lies in the fact that although we cannot inscribe ourselves in the book of long life, there is much we can do to try and write ourselves in the book of good life. For it is at least partly within our power to determine how we live, whether we do so more or less honestly, whether we care passionately for others or care not at all. Surely the book, if it is of any worth, will record our love and our striving, not just the length of time for which we existed. We therefore turn to God because God knows, and helps us to know, our faults, because God is the source and inspiration of all life and there is nothing else that can so help us to live well.

JONATHAN WITTENBERG

IN SEARCH OF LIFE

Every person merits life in accordance with the intensity of their attachment to the Holy, Blessed One. For it is written: '[God] breathed into [Adam's] nostrils the breath of life'. This means that the human being should be a vessel to breath in and draw forth life from the One who is the life source of all life.

RABBI YEHUDAH ARYEH LEV OF GUR: SEFAT EMET

ONCE I BELIEVED

Once I believed some grey and giant judge
kept careful toll of all the deeds of men,
that with some black and lasting kind of
pen
He cautiously recorded every petty crime,
and most of all – mine.

Now I know there is no judge with angry
pen
who bothers keeping track of all our deeds
and time;
Instead, each face records what life has
been about,
and sculpts a memory with every crack
and line,
and most of all – on mine.

JAMES KAVANAUGH

Our Father, our King, be gracious to us and answer us, though we have no merits

AVINU MALKENU

Each sentence in this prayer of supplications begins with the words Avinu Malkenu (Our Father! Our King!). God is described as the merciful father full of compassion for his children. But religious faith to be at all meaningful must present a constant challenge, calling out the best in its adherents. Hence God is described, too, as the king who makes demands on his subjects, and for whom his subjects have feelings of reverence and awe. The origin of the prayer is in the Talmudic account of how the great Akiba used the words in his request for rain: 'Our Father! Our King! We have no King besides thee. Our Father! Our King! Have mercy upon us! Our Father! Our King! Act unto us for thy name's sake!' Later on many additional verses were added but we cannot say with any degree of certainty when the prayer assumed its present form.

LOUIS JACOBS

Avinu Malkenu is such a simple prayer, such an elemental prayer, such a basic prayer! It contains all of the deepest hopes of our people: for health, for sustenance, for safety, for peace, for life. It started out in Talmudic times as a prayer that was said in time of drought and then, down through the ages, the people added lines to it, spelling out what they needed and what they feared the most.

Avinu Malkenu, the salutation, is a two-part definition of God. He is close to us, like a father; He is high above us, like a king. Not either/or, but both. 'King' stands for justice; 'Father' stands for mercy. 'King' stands for the fact that we are called to account for what we do in this world; 'Father' stands for the fact that there is mercy if we change.

Our Father, our King, we have sinned before you. It starts with this. Without saying this, the rest of the day is a waste. It is hard to say these words. It is hard to acknowledge that we have done wrong. 'I have sinned and I am sorry' are the hardest words in the language to pronounce, but say them we must. And once we do, how much lighter, how much cleaner, do we feel!

JACK RIEMER

A STORY BEFORE AVINU MALKENU

Nowadays it is our custom to sing the last lines of Avinu Malkenu out loud. There is a special melody for this line that everyone knows. It has become one of the most familiar songs of the High Holy Day Services.

But in Eastern Europe, the custom was to sing all the rest of the Avinu Malkenus out loud and the last line was said in silence. The Dubner Maggid was once asked why, and he explained, as was his way, with a parable.

Once there was a village grocer. Once a year he would go to the big city to order supplies and merchandise for the coming year. When he entered the warehouse he was dazzled by the amount and the variety of the merchandise that was on display there. And so he would say: 'Give me some of this' and 'Give me some of that.' He got carried away and he would go down the aisles ordering everything in sight. And then, when he got to the cashier and they totalled his bill he was embarrassed and he would say in a whisper: 'I am sorry but I don't have enough money with which to pay for all these things that I have ordered. Would you please give them to me on credit, and if I have a good year I will be able to pay for them all.'

And so it is with us, said the Dubner. When we think of all the things we would like to have in the new year we are overwhelmed with desire. And so we call out: Avinu Malkenu, give us health: Avinu Malkenu, give us wealth, etc., etc. But when we come to the last sentence and we realise how little merit we have, we say in a whisper: Avinu Malkenu, have pity on us and give us all we ask for on credit, even though we have no good deeds with which to pay for them. Give us another year of life and we will try to be better and to justify your faith in us and to pay you back for all you give us.

It is in that spirit that we should pray: Avinu Malkenu.

JACK RIEMER

Then all that has been made will know that it is You who made it, and every creature understand that You created it

THE VISION

On Rosh Hashanah we are called upon to appreciate the wonder of God's creation. But we are also recalled to the task of recreation, of the restoration of the spoilt and injured world so that it may become what it always was in the divine vision: a sacred place where none shall hurt and none destroy for everyone will recognise the presence of God.

We were not responsible for making the world, but we are for helping to remake and repair it. Nowhere is this taught more fiercely than in the prophetic readings for this season: We are party to God's vision and must be partners in its fulfilment:

> Is not this the fast I have chosen;
> that you loosen the fetters of evil,
> undo the bonds of the yoke,
> send forth free the oppressed
> and whatever the yoke, that you break it?
>
> Is it not that you share your bread with the hungry
> and bring home the wandering poor;
> that seeing the naked you cover them
> and do not hide from your own flesh?
>
> Then shall your light break forth like the dawn
> and your healing quickly spring up;
> then shall your righteousness go before you
> and the glory of the Lord gather you up. (Isaiah 57: 6–9)

JONATHAN WITTENBERG

REIGN OVER THE WHOLE UNIVERSE

This ancient benediction is part of each Amidah on Rosh Hashanah. Its theme, like that of so many other prayers of the day, is God as King. There is a nice comment on the Hebrew opening of this prayer which really means: 'Reign over the whole of all the universe.' The interpretation is based on the idea that in Jewish teaching a majority is treated as the whole. If, for instance, a majority of scholars favour a certain ruling the decision is given in their favour as if all the scholars were agreed. But the Jew is not content that the majority of men recognise God. He prays that God may reign over the whole of all the universe, he cannot rest until the idols are shattered and God alone is King. But, Jewish teachers remind us, world betterment must start with self betterment. Sublime though the idea of God's universal reign is, Jewish teaching is insistent that we start with ourselves.

LOUIS JACOBS

A STORY BEFORE WE BEGIN

I went to the hospital yesterday. There I found a man from out of town, whose wife is seriously ill. The man sits there day and night, next to her bed, with nothing to do and no one to talk to. I felt for him and so I did what I could to give him some strength.

The man told me that he is not a believer. In fact, he said to me, 'I have not been inside a synagogue in many years.'

I said to him: 'If you would like to come to services this year we would be glad to have you.' I told him that he would not need a ticket. He could just tell the usher that he was a guest of mine.

The man said to me: 'Look, Rabbi, whatever I have to ask of God, I can ask him from here.'

I said: 'That's true, but maybe God has something to ask of you.'

The man thought it over and said: 'I never thought of prayer that way.'

This is why we come to synagogue on Rosh Hashanah – not only to tell God what we need – God already knows what we need, at least as well as we do. We come to hear what God needs, to listen to his dreams, to hear his visions of the way the world should be, to find out what God wants to ask of us.

This is why we are here.

ARNOLD TURETSKY

The great Shofar is sounded and the voice of fine silence is heard

UNETANNEH TOKEF

This is probably the best known of the Yom Kippur hymns describing how God sits on his throne of justice and writes down the fate of all his creatures on Rosh Hashanah sealing the decree on Yom Kippur. The hymn concludes that 'Repentance, Prayer and Charity have the power of averting the evil decree.'

The hymn was composed by Meshullam ben Kalonymous, the author of many of the Yom Kippur hymns. Legend has it that the prayer was really composed by Rabbi Amnon of Mayence who, after his death, revealed it to Meshullam in a dream. According to this legend, Amnon resisted all the efforts of the Archbishop of Mayence to have him converted to Christianity. The Rabbi was tortured and his hands and feet cut off. As he was about to die he asked to be carried into the Synagogue. It was Yom Kippur and the congregation were about to recite the Kedushah prayer, the prayer of Sanctification of God's name. Rabbi Amnon recited the Unetanneh Tokef prayer, then expired. Most scholars, however, argue from the style and language of the meditation that, in fact, it originated at a much earlier date and that Meshullam simply added the final touches

While there is a certain grandeur about the meditation and while its popularity has been attested to throughout the ages it cannot be denied that if taken too literally the hymn can be offensive to modern tastes. Particularly the suggestion of repentance, prayer and charity as means of averting the divine threat of a horrible death 'by fire, by water, by the sword, by wild beasts, by earthquake, by plague, by strangling and by stoning' is hardly likely to prove the best incentive to the living of the good life. The problem of pain, the mystery of why the good God allows evil to exist, is one that has exercised the minds of the greatest religious thinkers. Various solutions have been offered but when all is said we have to confess defeat. We have to recognise that we are in the presence of the unfathomable, that the finite mind of man cannot hope to penetrate the secrets of the Infinite. But our faith insists on the belief in the goodness of God.

LOUIS JACOBS

OUR DEEDS DO NOT DISAPPEAR INTO THE BLACK HOLE OF TIME

The most dangerous enemy today is no longer the dark forces of totalitarianism, the various hostile and plotting mafias, but our own bad qualities. My presidential program is, therefore, to bring spirituality, moral responsibility, humaneness, and humility into politics, and, in that way, to make clear that there is something higher above us, that our deeds do not disappear into the black hole of time but are recorded somewhere and judged, that we have neither the right nor a reason to think that we understand everything and that we have the right to do everything.

ADDRESS OF PRESIDENT VACLAV HAVEL OF CZECHOSLOVAKIA
TO THE POLISH PARLIAMENT ON 21 JANUARY 1990

DOES DOING GOOD REALLY AVERT THE EVIL DECREE?

'Repentance, prayer and tsedakah avert the evil decree.' That is what the text says, but is it true? All of us know examples of people who have repented, who have prayed, and who have done acts of tsedakah, and yet have suffered. How then can we say these words?

It was Rabbi Nehemiah Nobel, the rabbi of Franz Rosenzweig, who explained the meaning of this line. He said: Notice that it does not say that these things *ma'avirin et hagezerah hara-ah*, which means 'avert the evil decree'. What it says is that they avert the *roa* of the *gezerah*, that they avert the evil of the decree. The decree comes to all people, to the good and to the bad alike. But those who live right, those who pray and repent and do tsedakah, are able to endure it better. They see themselves, not as the hub of the universe, but as spokes on God's wheel. They understand that God does not exist in order to serve us but that we exist in order to serve God. And so when the decree comes, as come it must to every person – they are able to accept it in faith.

JACK RIEMER

Thus says the Lord: 'I remember unto you the faithfulness of your youth, the love of your bridal days'

THE ADDITIONAL PRAYER

The Additional Amidah for Rosh Hashanah is more than a prayer, it contains the most sublime thoughts on God and his relationship to man; it is a summary of the Jewish faith and its cosmic significance in which are heard the accents of lawgiver, prophet and saint. The central feature of this Amidah is the recitation of Scriptural verses on the themes of divine Kingship, Remembrance and the sounding of the Shofar, each set of verses followed by an appropriate benediction. The three sets are known as Malchuyot (verses of Sovereignty), Zichronot (verses of remembrance) and Shofarot (verses dealing with the Shofar).

The arrangements of verses and benedictions in this form are very old but the order as we have it today (probably with some later additions) was composed by the famed Babylonian teacher, Rab (d. c.e. 247). Rab was born in Babylon, where Jews had lived for centuries and where they had risen to positions of power and affluence in the Persian Empire. Though mainly wealthy, and while playing its full share in maintaining Palestinian institutions and intensely loyal to Judaism, the Jewish Community in Babylon was not noted for its scholarship. Rab, like so many other keen students, left his home to sit at the feet of the renowned Palestinian teachers, particularly Rabbi Judah the Prince, the editor of the Mishnah, whose favourite pupil he became. Returning to Babylon, Rab stirred the intellectual sloth of his people. For more than eight hundred years Babylon became the foremost centre of Jewish learning in the world and this was attributed by later generations to the initial efforts of Rab. It was said that he found an open field and fenced it around. A giant of a man, physically as well as mentally so that he was given the nickname 'The Tall', he compelled the respect and reverence of his contemporaries and of subsequent generations. Among his sayings is that in the life to come there will be no eating or drinking, no procreation, no enmity or hatred, no competition, but the righteous will sit with their crowns on their heads basking in the radiance of the Divine Presence. Rab's family claimed descent from Shimei, the brother of King David. From the prayers he composed it can be seen that, in some measure, the mantle of the 'sweet singer in Israel' had, indeed, fallen upon him.

The Hebrew Bible is divided into three parts, *Torah*, the five books of Moses, *Nevi'im*, 'The Prophets', the prophetical and historical books, and *Ketubim* 'The Sacred Writings', Psalms, Proverbs, Job and so forth.

This division is followed in the Malchuyot, Zichronot and Shofarot arrangement. The structure of each of these is first a hymn of adoration, expressing the idea of Sovereignty, Remembrance or the Shofar, followed by Biblical texts on the same theme. These texts are ten in number, the first three from the *Torah*, the second three from the *Ketubim* (actually from the psalms), and the third set of three from the

Nevi'im, followed by a final *Torah* text. Each set of ten concludes with an appropriate benediction.

LOUIS JACOBS

The Holy One, blessed be He, said:
Say before me on Rosh Hashanah
prayers about kingship, remembrance
and the Shofar:
about kingship so that you proclaim me
your king,
about remembrance so that the
remembrance of you comes before me
for good,
and as for how to do this, do it with the
Shofar!

TALMUD: ROSH HASHANAH 16A

MALCHUYOT

What distinguishes the Days of Awe from all other festivals of the year is that here – and only here – does the Jew kneel. Here he does what he refused to do before Haman, what no power on earth could compel him to do, and what he need not do before God on any other day of the year, or in any other situation he may face during his lifetime. And he does not kneel to confess a fault, or to pray for forgiveness of sins. He kneels only in beholding the immediate nearness of God.

FRANZ ROSENZWEIG

ZICHRONOT

At the heart of the Rosh Hashanah service lie the Zichronot prayers. Their theme is memory, but not memories of the dead or recollections of events gone by. Rather, they remind us of the bond, of the love between ourselves and God. In the long history of our relationship nothing is forgotten. Images of the tenderness, but also of the fierce fidelity, of human love reawaken in us the force of the pact between us and remind us, on both sides, to meet the responsibilities entailed by our bond.

JONATHAN WITTENBERG

SHOFAROT

Not one part of the ram which Abraham sacrificed in place of his son Isaac went to waste. Its ashes formed the base of the inner altar on which the High Priest made atonement for all Israel once each year. Its sinews were ten, corresponding to the ten sinews of David's harp. With its skin Elijah girded his loins. As for its two horns, the left horn was blown at Mount Sinai, as it is said: 'The voice of the Shofar grew stronger and stronger' (Exodus 19: 19). The right horn, which is greater than the left, will be blown in the future at the time of the ingathering of the exiles, as it is said: 'On that day the great Shofar shall be blown; all those lost in the land of Assyria and all those outcast in the land of Egypt will come and worship the Lord at the holy mountain in Jerusalem' (Isaiah 27: 13).

BASED ON PIRKEI D'RABBI ELIEZER 31

All Vows, Prohibitions, Pledges and Oaths . . .

כל נדרי ואסרי וחרמי, וקונמי וכנויי, וקנסי ושבועת

KOL NIDREI

A man's word is sacred. This is the idea behind the vow. A promise must be kept. In Biblical times a vow might be made to carry out a certain act or to abstain from carrying out a certain act, generally for the purpose of self-discipline, e.g. a vow to abstain from wine or strong drink. Some of the Rabbis favoured the attempt at reinforcement of one's resolutions for good by means of the vow but others looked upon it with disapproval. 'It is sufficient for thee that which the Torah forbids' is a typical Talmudic saying.

The Talmud rules that a declaration made at the beginning of the year cancelling all vows that will be made during the coming year has the effect of rendering those vows null and void. In due course (before the ninth century) a special formula, the Kol Nidrei (Kol = all, Nidrei = the vows), was introduced in Aramaic, the vernacular of the day. Despite much opposition on the part of many scholars the formula came to stay. The haunting melody which gives the Kol Nidrei its tremendous appeal is of uncertain, but later, origin. The bitter years of Jewish persecution, the degradation of sin, the hope of repentance, the yearning of the estranged soul for reconciliation with God, all these find their expression in the melody. It has been noted that the tune possesses three motifs – first a note of pain and remorse, then a note of resolution and finally a note of triumph, corresponding to the three stages of repentance.

Jewish law does not know of the annulment of vows and promises made to others. The Kol Nidrei has reference only to private vows, to promises affecting the self, e.g. a promise to abstain from food. Yet throughout the ages ignorant Jew-haters have claimed that the oath of the Jew was unreliable because he annuls all his vows with the Kol Nidrei formula. Bigotry in this way justified the introduction of the infamous *more Judaico*, a special form of oath for the Jew in the Law Courts of the Middle Ages. A Byzantine law of the tenth century required a Jew while swearing to have a girdle of thorns round his loins and to stand in water. By a German code Jews had to stand on a sow's hide while taking the oath, and in the fifteenth century the law of Silesia required him to stand 'on a three-legged stool, pay a fine each time he falls, and lose his case if he falls four times'.

In view of these facts, Dr J. H. Hertz was undoubtedly right when he argued that for Jews to give up the recitation of the Kol Nidrei on the grounds of misunderstandings it gives rise to is for them tacitly to admit that the Jew-baiters were right that our ancestors' word was not to be trusted.

LOUIS JACOBS

THE MUSIC OF KOL NIDREI

The opening notes of the Kol Nidrei melody are instantly evocative of the most important evening service in the Jewish year. Perhaps it is the only occasion for some for synagogue attendance but the repetition, three times, of those falling cadences combined with the solemnity of the evening, fixes them in the Jewish sub conscious. The earliest record of the famous Ashkenazi music is from the sixteenth century, although the prayer dates from much earlier. Traditionally it is recited three times starting quietly and gradually getting louder. The minor mode gives way to the more positive major at the words 'may it come to us for good'. The Sephardim have their own tune. The 'Kol Nidrei' theme has inspired composers by its beauty. Beethoven had been studying Jewish liturgical music and used the theme in his C sharp minor quartet. Max Bruch, who was not Jewish, made the well-known setting for cello. Schoenberg composed his version of the prayer in 1938, after escaping to the United States, as a reaction to the anti-Semitism in Germany.

JUDY OBRART

ALL VOWS

All vows, promises, and commitments
made in your presence –
May we be given the strength to keep
them:

Our vows to ourselves, commitments to
self-discipline –
May we take our own lives seriously
enough to heed them,
Honouring our resolves in the way we
eat and drink,
The way we work and rest, the way we
regulate our lives.

Commitments made to loved ones and
friends,
Pledges made to worthwhile causes –
Help us to become as compassionate and
generous
As we sought to be at those noble
moments.

The promises we made to study and to
worship –
We meant them when we made them,
But distractions were many, and our
wills were weak.
This time, may we be strong enough;
May our better selves prevail.

Promises made in the synagogue by young
people
Who glimpsed what life as Jews might hold
in store for them,
May devotion and idealism be with them
all their days.

Our marriage vows – may they endure
Through dark days and through dull days,
Through fatigue and through
frustration –
May our love prove strong and our faith
firm.

O God, we meant the promises we made
To You, to each other, and to ourselves,
Even as we mean the vows we silently make
tonight.

Reach down to us as we strive to reach
up toward you;
Give us strength and self-respect, the
fidelity and vision,
To grow to become the people we have
sworn to be.

All worthy vows and commitments which
we make
From this Yom Kippur until the next
May we be faithful enough and firm
enough to keep them.

HAROLD KUSHNER

Do not cast us out from Your presence; do not take Your holy spirit away from us

SHEMA KOLENU: HEAR OUR VOICE

It is not known who combined the line from the daily liturgy with the verses which now form the familiar Shema Kolenu, or exactly when they did so. The sequence was once probably no more than just one among many components of the penitential service. Perhaps it is the melody that has made this short piece into one of the most moving and memorable of our prayers.

The theme is simple and speaks to everyone: we call to God to hear us and be near us through all the tribulations of life. We ask God to accept our prayer, but we do not specify what that prayer is because we can't. It is the sum of all our longings, both those which we have expressed in words elsewhere and those which cannot be articulated but are felt in the heart. It amounts to the one petition that God will not reject us, that, happen what may, God will not withdraw the sacred spirit from us.

Herein lies the dignity, purpose and wonder of being human. For, though at a basic level life may be no more than a physical function, all of us are privileged with the capacity to recognise, live by and carry with us the sacred spirit of God who gave it to us. This is our purpose: to find that spirit in ourselves, to respect and love it in others and to listen to its quiet voice in all our actions. With it we will manage even the worst things; without it we are abandoned in a loud, chaotic world without a guide. Therefore we say 'Bring us back to You, O Lord' and be with us thereafter. Admonish us if need be for 'thy rod and thy staff, they comfort me'. But never cast us off.

JONATHAN WITTENBERG

A PRAYER FOR THE CHILDREN

We pray for the children who put chocolate fingers on everything, who love to be tickled, who stomp in puddles and ruin their new pants, who eat candy before supper and who can never find their shoes in the morning.

And we also pray for those who stare at photographers from behind barbed wire, who have never bound down the street in a new pair of shoes, who have never played 'one potato, two potatoes' and who are born in places that we would not be caught dead in and that they will be.

We pray for the children who give us sticky kisses and fistfuls of dandelions, who sleep with their dog and who bury their goldfish, who hug us so tightly and who forget their lunch money, who squeeze toothpaste all over the sink, who watch their fathers shave, and who slurp their soup.

And we also pray for those who will never get dessert, who have no favourite blanket to drag around behind them, who watch their fathers suffer, who cannot find any bread to steal, who do not have any rooms to clean up, whose pictures are on milk cartons instead of on dressers, and whose monsters are real.

We pray for the children who spend all of their allowance by Tuesday, who pick at their food, who love ghost stories, who shove dirty clothes under the bed and who never rinse the bathtub, who love visits from the Tooth Fairy, even after they find out who it really is, who do not like to be kissed in front of the school bus, and who squirm during services.

And we also pray for those children whose nightmares occur in the daytime, who will eat anything, who have never seen a dentist, who are not spoiled by anyone, who go to bed hungry and wake up hungry, who live and move and have no address. We pray for those children who like to be carried and for those children who have to be carried, for those who give up and for those who never give up, for those who will grab the hand of anyone kind enough to offer it and for those who find no hand to grab.

For all these children, Adonai, we pray today, for they are all so precious.

INA J. HUGHS

And for the sin we have sinned before You out of confusion of heart

THE CONFESSIONAL PRAYERS

The value of confession is obvious. The wrongdoer feels a pressing need not alone to make good the wrong he has done but to express contrition. The Rabbis teach that confession of sin is an integral part of true repentance. They disapproved of confessing sins to a human being. God alone was to be the recipient of admissions of human failure. True, here and there in the moralistic literature, especially among the medieval mystics known as the Hasidim of Ashkenaz we find the advice given to confess one's shortcomings to a trusted friend but, on the whole, it is safe to say that Judaism has nothing corresponding to the idea of confession to a priest with powers of absolution.

Originally there was no fixed formula of confession. Each person on Yom Kippur confessed to any sins he had committed during the past year. In the course of time two fixed formulas were adopted – *Ashamnu* and *Al Het.* The alphabetical acrostic form of these two confessions has puzzled many. Does this not reduce the whole of the confession to a purely mechanical act devoid of inwardness? The usual answer is that in the days before the invention of printing such devices were essential if the prayers were to be remembered. There is, too, much point in the observation that where the congregation adopts the same form of confession the individual is spared embarrassment if his confession is overheard. In Temple times, the Rabbis teach, the sin offering was slaughtered in the same place as other offerings in order not to put the sinner to shame.

Another difficulty mentioned in a number of sources is what should a man do if he is sure that he has never in his life been guilty of some of the offences enumerated in the two formal confessions? Many teachers refer in this connection to the doctrine that each Israelite is responsible for the sins of his fellows. Though the idea of collective responsibility can be over-stressed there is much in the thought that the good man sets an example of goodness while the wrongdoer lowers the standard and makes it more difficult for others to do the right thing.

There, is, too, the idea that for the greater man a minor sin is comparable to a major transgression of a lesser person for the greater man ought to know better. This is behind such Rabbinic teachings as that he who flies into a rage is as one who worships idols. Seen in this light the whole list of sins is applicable to each one, for even where a man is not guilty of infringement in a gross sense he may be held culpable for a sin akin to the original prohibition.

LOUIS JACOBS

WHY DO WE CONFESS TO SINS WE HAVE NOT DONE?

Over and over we repeat a litany of sins, the repetition digging deeper into our souls each time and, progressively, uncovering the reality of our failings. Words spur self-discovery.

Yet the list of sins to which the congregation confesses clearly contains misdeeds not committed by most of the congregation. Why should a worshipper stand before God and ask forgiveness for transgressions that he or she never committed?

The first answer is that this acts as a shield for those who need to confess. When all the congregation lift up their voices and say 'We have sinned by . . . ' no one knows who is truly confessing to the misdeed.

There is another, deeper reason. We tend to split ourselves off from those who commit terrible crimes. They seem different in kind. Sometimes this protects us, sometimes it simply serves as an excuse. We turn criminals into monsters and therefore we need not share the sense that they, too, are people. Yet it is precisely the violation of what we share that is so horrible.

Judaism teaches that those who commit terrible deeds are not monsters. They are human beings who have done monstrous things. If they were beasts, they would be blameless. They are human, and responsible because they have betrayed their humanness.

We share humanity. It would be possible for us to commit those same terrible crimes in certain situations if we allowed ourselves to do it. Therefore we are not allowed to say, 'Well, given my character, I could never do such a thing.' By confessing to sins we have not committed, we admit that such deeds are possible for us. We do not separate ourselves. We recognise the demonic potential that exists in the most placid breast.

DAVID WOLPE

AND FOR THE SIN OF TIMIDITY

The last of the sins on the list is: for the sin that we have committed against you, *b'timhon levav* – out of timidity. How many are the sins that we commit, not out of greed and not out of envy, and not out of evil intention, but simply out of cowardice? We are afraid to stand out in the crowd, to be moral when those around us are not, for fear of being laughed at or called religious. And so we go along with what we know inside is just not right. We conform but deep down we know that this is not the way we should be living. And so, at least once a year, we confront our cowardice, and pray that we may have the strength and the courage and the self-esteem to do what we know is right, and not go along with wrongdoing out of timidity.

JACK RIEMER

The dust returns to the earth as it was, But the spirit returns to God who gave it

THE MEMORIAL SERVICE FOR THE DEPARTED

The idea of praying for the souls of the departed is ancient. In the second book of the Maccabees it is said that Judah collected the sum of two thousand drachmas of silver and sent it to Jerusalem as a sin offering for those who had died 'in that he was mindful of the resurrection. For if he had not hoped that they that were slain should have risen again, it had been superfluous and vain to pray for the dead. And also in that he perceived that there was great favour laid up for those that died godly, it was an holy and good thought. Whereupon he made a reconciliation for the dead, that they might be delivered from sin.'

That the living can atone by their charity for those who have died is found in a number of passages in the Rabbinic literature. Arising out of this belief it became customary to recite special prayers for the dead and to donate to charity on their behalf on Yom Kippur. At first these prayers were recited on Yom Kippur only (the Torah reading for Yom Kippur morning begins with the words: 'And the Lord spake unto Moses after the death of the two sons of Aaron . . . ')

In the order of prayers known as Mahzor Vitri (1208) reference is made to memorial prayers on Yom Kippur, not on the other festivals. But at a later date the custom arose of reciting these prayers on all festival days on which the portion of the Torah dealing with the duty of supporting the poor is read, namely on the last days of Passover and Pentecost and on the eighth day of Tabernacles.

The central idea behind the Memorial Service is that a person's life does not come to an end with the death of his body. His soul lives on in two ways. First, Judaism teaches that the soul of man is immortal, that after his bodily death it continues to exist and that therefore what we do with our lives is of eternal significance. And secondly, the soul of a man who has influenced others lives on, here on earth, even when he has gone to his eternal rest. By remembering their parents in the Memorial Prayer, sons and daughters keep their memory alive by resolving to follow in their teachings.

LOUIS JACOBS

A LAST LETTER

Vera and her sister Eva were sent by their parents from their happy childhood home to England after the Nazi invasion of Czechoslovakia in 1939. The family was never to be reunited. Vera and Eva's father was taken away in 1943. Their mother survived the war, first in Terezin and then at Belsen. The news that she was alive reached her children but was soon followed by bitter disappointment: she died of typhus soon after the liberation. Below is part of a letter she wrote to her daughters in the knowledge that she would shortly be deported. She left it with

וישב העפר על הארץ כשהיה,
והרוח תשוב אל האלהים אשר נתנה

a family friend who gave it to Vera when she visited her home town in the summer of 1945.

My dearest children – My life belonged to you, and you and your dear father were the happiness of my life. If only this letter were not to say goodbye, if only fate, which has treated me so cruelly, would once more allow me to be reunited with you and the one we all so dearly love, if only we could resume our life together, life filled with joy and love . . .

When I was sixteen years old I met your father. Never did I think that one person could give so much love and happiness. My life turned into the most joyful dream, the most wonderful fairy tale. When we were married on 12 December 1920, I was the happiest person alive. Four perfect years went by and then you arrived, Evicko, who are nineteen years old today, to whom I should like to say so many beautiful things, but to whom – and to my dear Veruska – I am now writing this sad letter, yet hoping that one day I may be able to tell you everything, to hold you close to my anguished heart

On 13 November, two days after your father's birthday, I was numbed by the cruel blow which fate dealt me – and you – my dearest children, on that day . . .

They took away your father, your good, kind father who took such good care of us, whose only wish was your happiness, who so hoped to be reunited with you one day, who so looked forward to that day; he lived for you, he had faith in you, and he believed – so very very much . . .

Your father and I wanted to live, work and suffer together, and now they have torn us apart. I promise you, my dear children, that I shall be brave, that the thought of you and of our dearest one will be my strength and that I shall not give up – but will fate allow me to see happier days?

This letter will be given to you; always hold these friends in high esteem and never forget their goodness.

And now, my dear children, on behalf of your father and myself, I wish you – not only for the new year, not only for Eva's birthday, but for the rest of your life . . . Be happy, be brave. We gave you love, we gave you the foundations of life, we wanted to give you more, so much more . . . How I wish that fate would make up to you all it has refused us, how I hope that your life will flow smoothly, filled with joy and happiness. Remember your home and us, but do not grieve. Your whole life lies before you, life which you will build at the side of your husbands. I give my blessing to them and to your children; I shall be watching over you from Heaven, and praying for your happiness.

I embrace you and I bless you,

Your maminka.

FROM VERA GISSING: *PEARLS OF CHILDHOOD*

And thus he used to say: O Lord, Your people the house of Israel have sinned, transgressed and done wrong before You

THE AVODAH

The Avodah (service, Temple worship) is the order of worship of the Israelites in the Temple. It is related during the Yom Kippur Musaph service in order to recall former glories and to re-enact symbolically the ancient rites. The descriptive verses by Meshullam ben Kalonymous are based on the Talmudic accounts.

The first paragraph of the Avodah speaks of God creating all things, of the creation of Adam and Eve, of their sin, of Cain and Abel, of Noah, Abraham, Isaac and Jacob, of Jacob's son Levi, from whom the High Priest, the hero of the day, was descended. Then begins the account of the preparations for the great day of worship and of the service itself.

The High Priest made confession three times – once for himself, once for his household and the priests, and once for all the congregation of Israel. When making these confessions he would pronounce the 'glorious and awful name', i.e. the ineffable name of God which could not be pronounced at any other time and when the people and the priests heard it they fell upon their faces. When the Reader and congregation refer to the priests and the people prostrating themselves they, too, fall to the ground on their knees and touch the ground with their faces. The account concludes with the prayer the High Priest recited when he came forth in safety from the Holy of Holies (the tradition has it that if the High Priest were unworthy he would not survive his entry into the sacred spot on such a day). The prayer ends with the plea that the houses of the inhabitants of the plain of Sharon, built on shifting sands, may not become their graves.

LOUIS JACOBS

וכך היה אומר : אנא השם , חטאו , עוו ,
פשעו לפניך עמך בית ישראל

PRELUDE TO THE AVODAH SERVICE

The whole world of the Holy One is magnificent and holy. In the holy land, the Land of Israel, the holiest city is Jerusalem. In ancient Jerusalem the holiest place was the Temple and the holiest place in the Temple was the Holy of Holies.

Among all people in the world the Jews are bound to the Land of Israel. The holiest group among the Jews was the tribe of the Levites. The holiest of the Levites were the priests and among them the holiest was the High Priest.

The holiest of all things written in the holy tongue of Hebrew is the Torah. The holiest part of the Torah is the Ten Commandments, and the holiest word in the Ten Commandments is God's Divine Name.

In all the year the holiest days are the holidays. The holiness of the Sabbath surpasses that of the holidays, and the holiest Sabbath is Yom Kippur, the Sabbath of Sabbaths.

Once each year these four supreme holinesses – of place, people, language and time – were joined. On Yom Kippur, the High Priest entered the Holy of Holies and uttered God's Divine Name. And as this moment was holy and awesome beyond human conception, it held great potential danger for the High Priest and for the Jewish people, for had the High Priest met with an obstacle at that time, through a wayward or sinful thought which could lead his mind astray, for example, the entire world hanging in the balance under judgment could have been destroyed.

Wherever a man stands with his heart directed to heaven is a Holy of Holies. Every day in a person's life is Yom Kippur. Every Jew is a High Priest. And every word spoken in purity and holiness is God's Divine Name. Every destructive thought that we nurture, every moral catastrophe, could cause the whole world to collapse.

FROM SH. ANSKY: *THE DYBBUK*, ADAPTED FROM
BIALIK'S TRANSLATION BY JULES HARLOW

These things do I remember and pour out my soul within me, for strangers have devoured us

ELEH EZKERAH – THESE THINGS DO I REMEMBER

The Roman Emperor Hadrian, resolved to stamp out Judaism ruthlessly, engaged on a bloody persecution during which many of Israel's sages perished. In those days numerous Jewish families gave their lives for the Sabbath, circumcision and other Jewish institutions. Tradition records that ten great sages were slain during the Hadrianic persecutions. Later legend describes how they were all killed on the same day, though this is historically incorrect. This dirge in the Yom Kippur liturgy is based on a late Midrash and describes the martyrdom of the ten sages in detail.

No mention is made here of the Hadrianic persecutions. Instead it is said that the Emperor, after reading in the Torah the account of Joseph and his brothers, asked the Sages the punishment for one who steals a man. When they answered that he was to be sentenced to death the Emperor ordered them to be put to death to expiate the sin of Joseph's brothers, their ancestors. Ishmael inquired in Heaven if this were indeed to be their fate and he was told that they must be prepared to die. The theology of the dirge is inconsistent with the general Jewish view that descendants do not suffer for the sins of their ancestors. Because of this difficulty and the anachronisms in the dirge Dr H. J. Zimmels is of the opinion that the whole lament is a veiled attack on the Church which persecuted the Jews.

Among the ten martyrs were Akiba who died with a smile on his lips in obedience to the verse: 'And thou shalt love thy God with all thy life', which Akiba interpreted to mean: 'Even if thy life is demanded', and Hananiah ben Teradion who was burned at the stake with a Sefer Torah wrapped round his body and who said that he saw 'the parchments burning but the letters of the Torah flying aloft'.

LOUIS JACOBS

WE STAND BEFORE OUR GOD

In 1935, when anti-Semitism was rampant throughout Germany, Rabbi Leo Baeck (1873–1956) who was the president of the representative organisation of German Jewry, wrote this prayer which was distributed to all rabbis in the country for reading at Kol Nidrei services.

In this hour all Israel stands before God, the judge and the forgiver.

In his presence let us all examine our ways, our deeds, and what we have failed to do.

Where we transgressed, let us openly confess: 'We have sinned!' and, determined to return to God, let us pray: 'Forgive us.'

With the same fervour with which we confess our sins, the sins of the individual and the sins of the community, do we, in indignation and abhorrence, express our contempt for the lies concerning us and the defamation of our religion and its testimonies.

We have trust in our faith and in our future.

Who made known to the world the mystery of the Eternal, the One God?

Who imparted to the world the comprehension of purity of conduct and purity of family life?

Who taught the world respect for man, created in the image of God?

Who spoke of the commandment of righteousness, of social justice?

In all this we see manifest the spirit of the prophets, the divine revelation to the Jewish people. It grew out of our Judaism and is still growing. By these facts we repel the insults flung at us.

We stand before our God. On him we rely. From him issues the truth and the glory of our history, our fortitude amidst all change of fortune, our endurance in distress.

Our history is a history of nobility of soul, of human dignity. It is history we have recourse to when attack and grievous wrong are directed against us, when affliction and calamity befall us.

God has led our fathers from generation to generation. He will guide us and our children through these days.

We stand before our God, strengthened by his commandment that we fulfil. We bow to him and stand erect before men. We worship him and remain firm in all vicissitudes. Humbly we trust in him and our path lies clear before us; we see our future.

All Israel stands before her God in this hour. In our prayers, in our hope, in our confession, we are one with all Jews on earth. We look upon each other and know who we are; we look up to our God and know what shall abide.

'Behold, He that keepeth Israel doth neither slumber nor sleep.' (Psalm 121: 4)

'May he who maketh peace in his heights bring peace upon us and upon all Israel.'

FROM N. GLATZER,
THE DYNAMICS OF EMANCIPATION

Open unto us the gate at the hour of the closing of the gate, for day has declined

FROM THE LAWS OF NEILAH

The time for the Neilah prayer is when the sun is in the treetops, so that it is completed at sunset . . .

Instead of 'write us in the book of life', one says 'seal us in the book of life.'

SHULKHAN ARUCH: ORACH HAYYIM 623: 2

For at Neilah the decree written for each person on Rosh Hashanah is sealed for good or for bad. One should therefore make a great effort in this prayer, for the culmination of the ten days of penitence is Yom Kippur and the culmination of Yom Kippur is Neilah. For everything depends on the conclusion, for 'if not now, when?'[1] Therefore, even if one is weak from fasting, one should nevertheless gird oneself like a warrior and pray with pure, clear concentration, accepting upon oneself the practices of repentance. For 'the one who comes to be purified will surely find help'[2] and be sealed in the book of good life.

MISHNAH BERURAH

NOTE 1. The quotation is from Hillel in the Chapters of the Fathers (1: 14). Later in the work the same scholar is quoted as saying: Don't say 'when I have time I'll do it', lest you never have time (2.5). The opportunity is always now. Nowhere is this more apparent than at Neilah: the gates are about to close, there is no time to waste.

NOTE 2. The source of this saying is in the Talmud (Yoma 38b). Wherever we may be coming from we should not think that we will have to make the journey home to our people and our God alone and unsupported. Only we can begin, but as soon as we do so our resolve will be strengthened and our path illumined.

NEILAH

In Temple times deputations of laymen were delegated to be present each day when the priests offered up the sacrifices on behalf of Israel. Towards the end of the day when the Temple gates were about to be shut these men would recite the Prayer of the closing of the Gates (Neilat Shearim – Neilah = 'to close'). On fast days this special concluding service was added to the prayers of the day but in the course of time this addition was reserved for Yom Kippur. At a later period it was natural to associate the idea of the closing gates with the gates of Heaven open to prayer during the long day. The note sounded at Neilah is one of hope. The sun is about to set, the prayers have ascended on high, Israel has become reconciled to its God. The traditional melodies express the mood of longing, of yearning for a better life, of triumph over sin.

LOUIS JACOBS

OPEN THE GATES

Open for us the gates
Even as the gates are being closed.
The sun is low, the hour is late,
Let us come into the gates at last.

In our lives many gates swing shut.

As a man begins life, it spreads before him like a corridor with many doors. But as he walks down this corridor the doors close behind him, one by one, year by year. This is a teaching of the Neilah service: Remember the unopened doors. Enter them before they close.

We live only once. Do we not want to live fully? The corridor of life stretches before us. Each one of us must perforce walk down its stately length. The gates do not stand open forever: as we walk down the corridor they shut behind us. And at the end they are all closed, except the one dark door that leads to the ultimate chamber of God. This then is the meaning of Neilah; the call to the doors which we never open. Before it is too late, let us open the gates that lead to truth, enter the door of beauty, go through the doors of goodness. Let us open the gates to those things in life which abide eternally – before the gates swing shut, before the doors are closed.

MILTON STEINBERG

עיונים

Reflections

1 For it is your life and the length of your days

DEUTERONOMY 30: 20

Two chains of thought are provoked, more or less inevitably, by the consciousness of the impending days. The first is concerned with who we are; the second with who we are not and never shall be.

God, our tradition teaches, sees to the heart. The requirements of atonement make us search the conscience. More practically, more down to earth than these inward matters, the very fact of the passing of the year calls us to account with its messengers, the sharp smell of the air in the colder mornings, the changing colour of the leaves and the visit to the family graves. What have I done since I was last here? What has happened to me since last I saw these things? So much has overtaken me! It has all gone so terribly fast! Struck by the swift dissipation of our time, we ask ourselves the questions which are also God's questions of us: Who are we and what is our life worth?

Just as deeply, often no less painfully, we are penetrated by thoughts of who we are not and never shall be and by memories of who we once were but cannot again become. We won't be young again, as we were last year or on that occasion thirty years ago, which seems as close in memory as a butterfly scarcely beyond grasp. We won't have back our pet, our friend, our parent, our partner who is gone. We won't rewrite the history of our marriage, or the marriage we didn't have. We will not be an engine driver, or a hero, or a person who has not given other people hurt and made painful and bad mistakes.

Such reflections may either undermine, or underline, our faith in life. Which?

As a rabbi it is one of the sadder parts of my work frequently to attend funerals. Any death is hard for the family to bear; all the more so if it is untimely. But, due chiefly to the courage and humanity of the people whose bereavements I have witnessed, it has never once occurred to me as I turned the car round to drive back home from the cemetery, that life is pointless, simply not worth the candle. On the contrary, again and again the same thought has come back to me: Life is short so use it well. Time will not repeat itself; make the most of it.

Life is short so live it to the full. If there is something good we want to do, something that brings happiness and is not greedy, careless or hurtful to another, then we should do it. Particularly if there is something we can do that will enhance our enjoyment, and that of others, of the beauty of the world, of its plants, trees, animals and birds, rivers, seas and mountains, then we should do it. If there is something which will augment our appreciation of the human spirit, through music, art or through simply meeting different people, then we should do it. So may the inevitable 'never more' not taste bitter when it comes, and the years be full of the honest privileges of life.

Life is short so use it well. If we have responsibilities that call us, a moral sense of how we ought to act, as Judaism teaches that we surely must have, then we have to heed them. We should not say: 'When I have time I'll turn aside;'[1] next month, or next year, or in the next decade I'll do what I know is right. We must involve ourselves now. We live in a world full of needs; they call to the conscience all the time. Why delay our response? Why fail to alleviate the small fragment of suffering about which we can indeed do something? Maybe in the future we will not have the capacities or the time. Maybe our heart will have grown hard. Why feel lethargic guilt at what we are not doing, when we could be fully occupied with what is right and good?

Life is short, a limited privilege, an opportunity bound. If ever in our spirit we have heard God's calling, let us follow it now. More than the investigation of our conscience, more than the appeal to acknowledge, regret and repent, these coming Days of Awe confront us with the wonder of existence in the presence of God who fills all the world. We may have sensed such Being only rarely, only once or twice in our whole life. Never matter; if the stars are not extinguished by a night of thick cloud, if the companionship of our own heart is not lost to us, despite long months of heedless alienation, how much less, then, can that Presence be shut away. Nothing so inflames vitality, nothing so engulfs the soul, as to seek it and be found.

There is, then, much we may regret concerning who we are, who we are not and who we never shall be. But, in considering these things, let them provoke in us not despondency but rather the realisation that there is far more that we can and may and should become, that life is calling to us with fresh poignancy at the renewal of the year.

1. Hillel: Chapters of the Fathers 2: 52

2 You stand this day, all of you, before the Lord your God

DEUTERONOMY 29: 9

The humdrum of our daily life constantly divides us. It separates us from each other through sheer lack of time, it separates us from ourselves through countless distractions. But in these sacred days and the mood of awe which fills them lies the power to reunite

Such promised harmony may seem at odds with the anxious irritability which precedes the High Holiday season in so many homes. It's a great time for family bad temper. There are good reasons for this. The fear of expectations makes us tense. There is the big Judgement. How do I stand before God? What will God see in my soul, and for what fortunes will God write me down? And there are the little judgements: How will I manage the long services and the fast? How will I cope with the relatives who're coming to stay, with the family's wants and needs? Whom have I offended? (Someone, no doubt.) Whom am I likely to offend? Will I get myself / my mother / my husband / wife / children to the Shul on time?

All these issues, some of them scarcely conscious, make us tense. Yet these days can, on the contrary, bring release from expectation. Here we may let go. We don't have to be the hamster-like person so many of us have almost involuntarily allowed ourselves to become, rushing round and round on a wheel just to stay where we are. We don't have to prove anything to anybody, to be successful, youthful or suave; we are not here to satisfy others or confirm the image of what we suppose we ought to be. A greater perspective causes these things to diminish and dissolve: We stand before God exactly as we are. After all, does God not know?

But it is not only the rush, there is also the incessant division of our selves into tiny pieces. For, in many of our lives, there is the work person, or the school person, and the home person, and the shopper and the cook and the driver and the friend who listens quietly, and the leisure person who (in the intervals between the above) is supposed to paint, play music, or keep the lawn cut short. Alternatively, or in addition, there is also the problem of having to pretend to be what we are not, busy when we are not, free when we are not, calm when we feel tense, confident when confused. But over these holidays these distractions can temporarily cease. The diffuse, discrepant parts of ourselves can, must, meet and come together. For it is all of us, the whole of us, that stands before our God.

This fact has the power to alter the perspective from which we regard our life and draw us back to who we most essentially are. To what may this change be compared? It is like walking round and down the curves of a steeply declining road. To the left and the right are high banks grown over with scrub and wind blown trees from which birds call. Suddenly, shockingly, although we knew it was there, the sea lies before us vast and bare, the rocks and coves of the shore, the white crests of the waves, the grey distance and the huge, undifferentiated horizon. In such a place the consciousness of our littleness unites in us all disparate thoughts. In such a place the words of the prayer are realised: 'Now, therefore, set the awe of You, O Lord our God, over all Your works, and the dread of You over all that You have made.' We forget the many diversions, we are reunited with our spirit.

Perhaps it is just this that frightens us and makes us apprehensive at the onset of the season. Who wants to stand undefended before the awesome God of all creation? Fragment us and distract us as it may, is not the familiar routine of our life preferable to such a prospect?

And yet, I believe, we meet this experience more with joy than with anxiety. For it has, if we let ourselves be challenged by it, the power to simplify and harmonise our lives. It helps us to reclaim our soul, reminding us of what really lies at the centre of our lives. It chastens our selfish purposes. It softens our hard heart. It restores our true, our innocent, vitality, small but real in the context of the infinite life that fills all things.

3 The great Shofar shall be sounded and the voice of fine silence heard

THE UNETANNEH TOKEF PRAYER

One reads in fairy tales of lovers whom fate or travels must divide. Prior to their parting they agree that once a year on the new moon of such and such a month at a certain hour they will think of one another, recalling all their adventures since last they met and remembering their love. Or it happens when someone dies that year after year the bereft partner returns to the grave and talks and communes with the loved one, preventing time from severing absolutely a bond that still has power to nourish life.

We and God, teaches the Rebbe of Slonim, Shalom Noach Brossovsky, are also beings separated. We are like a child whose parents have sent him on a long journey. Before he sets out they say to him: 'We must communicate regularly. However, letters, even messengers, are unreliable. Once a year, therefore, we must speak to one another directly.' God is the parent, we are the child, and the date for the meeting is Rosh Hashanah. The language by which we communicate is the sound of the Shofar.[1] More simply than words, its notes convey the contents of our heart to God who hears and knows. Thus the Shofar calls to God; but it also calls to us and to the memory of the bond between us which the fortunes of our bodily life inevitably cause us to forget yet which they cannot break.

The Shofar sounds and the brief communication begins. But what does one say at such a meeting, on such an occasion? What do long parted relatives say to one another, brothers and sisters, parents and children divided by tyranny and war? 'It's you!' one shouts with joy, and one thinks 'We're still here, you and I!' One remembers but a fraction of all that's happened and one feels: 'In spite of fate and fortune we've found each other once again!' One speaks incoherently, touching unintelligibly on all that's happened since last one met. Swiftly the events of the years flash by and, wanting to say everything at once, one lapses into silence. Then one remembers how much one has longed for this moment and starts to speak again. Thus, interrupting one another constantly, the two people spend their first moments reunited. That is what it's like with God and us. We speak and we say nothing, the Shofar is profound and inarticulate at once, it is both notes and silence. The mind is filled with awe that such a bond as this between our God and us exists, persists. What has our people not given, what would we not give, to be faithful to this bond? That is why our rabbis specified that the Shofar for Rosh Hashanah should be made of a ram's horn, recalling Isaac's binding, and all the sacrifices of our people ever since for the sake of keeping faith.

But after the first few minutes a second and more sombre mood overtakes the first, checking the excitement. It comes from the sense of unworthiness that now arises in the heart as we realise how often we have forgotten what matters most, how often trivialities have distracted us and unworthy preoccupations turned the heart aside. A wave of shame flows through us and sinks down into the soul: 'I have been careless'; 'I have not lived my life according to my best intuitions of truth and cleanliness'; 'I have been hurtful'. The images of cruel things we've done sure back at us with the gaze of a suffering animal, trapped in our brutality. 'How can I tell you about these things, God?' one thinks, 'yet how can I be near you and not tell?' We know that there is something we have damaged and fear lest in return we must forfeit our innocence forever. Rabbi Yossef Dov Soloveitchik compares the penitent with the mourner. The latter has lost a loved one, partner or parent; the former has lost himself. He weeps for his own soul and is ashamed.[2]

Yet precisely in that shame lies hope. For as a physical wound often elicits from the body those fluids that begin to heal it, so shame can adduce from the heart the cleansing power of remorse and the desire to do good.

This in turn leads to a third, conclusive, feeling: the resolve to be better in the future. 'Henceforth I shall be true!' That is what one says at the conclusion of the meeting: 'This time I won't forget! I will carry the thought of you with me wherever I go!' In that resolve is energy, courage and hope.

The last Tekiah ends; already the meeting is over. What have we actually said? Very little. Most probably our thoughts have been as inarticulate as the sounds of the Shofar. Yet that Shofar has called us home. Its notes, and the silence in between them, remind us, stir us, humble us and chasten us, and leave us with fresh purpose and new strength.

1 Rabbi Shalom Noach Brossovsky in *Sefer Netivot Shalom part 2,* Machon Emunah VaDa'at, Jerusalem 5749, pages 123–4

2 Rabbi Joseph Dov Soloveitchik in *Soloveitchik on Repentance,* edited by P. H. Peli, Paulist Press, New York / Ramsey 1984, page 196

4 Hayom Harat Olam: Today is the Birthday of the World. Today God puts on trial all creatures of all time

THE ROSH HASHANAH MUSAF SERVICE

Today is the anniversary of creation, today we celebrate the birthday of the world. Thus runs the general understanding of the familiar prayer: 'Hayom harat Olam'. But Rashi disagrees. 'Harat' comes not from a root connected with birth but from a word which means to tremble. On this day the world trembles; today is the anniversary of the first sin.

Between the poles of these two interpretations the drama of our lives, and of the world, is acted out. For creation is an act of trust; that which has been entrusted to us must be nurtured, cherished. Sin is an act of betrayal; what has been given to us is neglected, abused, destroyed. Whether or not we are faithful to the trust invested in us is a question which we answer in the way we live our lives. The fate of the world depends on our response.

Rosh Hashanah, 'the birthday of the world', brings this challenge home to us. But what does it mean to celebrate the renewal of creation? To answer this question we have to consider what difference it makes to think of the world as a created thing, rather than simply as eternal matter, as old as age itself.

The issue is not whether we believe the earth to be five thousand, seven hundred and fifty something years old. We do not have to pretend that dinosaurs are younger than they look; such matters do not threaten the tenets of our faith. To think of the world as God's creation means to respect this earth on which we are privileged to live and to honour the greater life to which it and we belong. It requires an appreciation of the fact that we may not do simply as we please. For when, according to the Torah, God breathed the breath of life into the first human beings and gave them free will and made them stewards over all creation, God showed a remarkable degree of trust. To celebrate creation on this 'birthday of the world' means, therefore, to keep faith with that great trust.

The concomitant of this is responsibility: to live in the world is to have a duty towards it. It is not ours to exploit to the bitter end. Just as Judaism teaches that I may not say that this is my life to do exactly what I like with, or even that this is my body to use entirely as I please, so we may not say that this is our earth to treat in whatever manner unbounded self interest dictates. For all these things are ours on trust only and for employment in a manner appropriate to our responsibilities. It is of this that Rosh Hashanah reminds us. Indeed, there are many to whom the question of the age of the world and precisely how it came into being are an absurd irrelevance, but who have a deep inner respect before its many forms of life and the sacred spirit which animates them and which they so diversely refract.

But to fulfil our responsibility is not easy, our life being a perpetual battle between heedlessness and concern, treachery and keeping faith.

Our rabbis encapsulate this drama in a

single telling image. God, as the Torah tells us, made garments for Adam and Eve. On these cloaks were portrayed all the birds of the air and the beasts of the field. Whenever any animal saw that cloak it felt an instant and total trust; it came and lay at Adam or Eve's feet. The garments were passed down to Noah who wore them to lure the representatives of every living being into the safety of the ark. But then, like so many precious but potentially dangerous things in our day, they fell into the wrong hands. Nimrod, the mighty hunter, became their owner. When he wore them the animals came as usual; there at his feet he put them to the slaughter.

The Nimrod of the twentieth century haunts us all.

Never in human history has it mattered so much to put off the garments of betrayal and put back on the garments of trust. That which is ruined, dirtied, polluted has become the image of our times. It has been said that the emblem of our age will be a starving child hugging a bird with its wings clogged in oil. Some consider us to be in need of a ritual that will enable us to mourn the loss of songbird and tree, clear river and pristine sea.

Let that not be the case. Instead let us take to heart the prayers of this festival of trust. Rather than lamenting, let us take hope from every example of trust unbroken or restored, from those who dedicate their lives to healing, both of persons and of places, and from those who in small but consistent acts of thoughtfulness eschew cruelty and keep faith with what is kind and good.

Let us resolve on this festival to make our contribution in turning treachery back to trust, trembling into celebration of the birthday of the world. Never has the hour been so urgent. Never has the world seemed smaller, or we so interdependent. Never has it been so clear that, in the words of Martin Luther King, 'we are caught in an inescapable network of mutuality, tied in a single garment of destiny'.[1]

For the trust which is at risk is the bond that spans creation, including plant and animal and human life, society, spirit and God.

1 Martin Luther King: Letter from Birmingham City Jail. In *The World Treasury of Modern Religious Thought*, edited by J. Pelikan, Little, Brown and Company, Boston, Toronto, London 1990, page 607.

5 Return, O Israel, unto the Lord your God . . . Take with you words, and return . . .

HOSEA 14: 2–3

'The Holy One, blessed be He, forgets, He hides His face, from the person who always insists on being right,' taught Rebbe Nachman of Breslav.[1] The first words we have to take with us on the journey of repentance are the words 'I have done wrong.'

Children say: 'The door hit me'; 'The table banged me'. Thus they make another the agent of their hurt. As grown-ups we are different; we have more sophisticated, more acceptable, ways of avoiding the admission of our mistakes: 'Something came over me'; 'I wasn't quite myself'; 'I don't know what got into me'. All these may be trivial circumlocutions, but who is the 'other' who gets into us, and are we wise to locate in him or her such inconvenient control over whom we really are? What, after all, can we do about someone else's faults? Would it not be better to let this 'other' in and admit that it too is part of us?

The Talmud (Chagigah 15a) tells the following sad story about Elisha ben Abbuya, known firstly to himself and then to others as 'Acher' or 'the other one' ever since he sinned and became an apostate. His friend and former pupil Rabbi Meir tries to persuade him to repent. Elisha objects, saying 'I have already heard them say behind the heavenly partition: 'Return O wayward children' – except for Acher!' Nevertheless, Rabbi Meir takes him to thirteen different Synagogues in an effort to bring him back to the right path. The houses of study are full of children and wherever they go Elisha asks one of them to recite the verse he is studying. In every case, all thirteen times, he hears a different reference to the impossibility of washing away sin. For Acher there is no hope.

But how can that be? Surely every one can repent! Is not the door always open? The answer lies in Rabbi Aharon Soloveitchik's brilliant but disturbing observation that Elisha ben Abbuya could of course return to God. So long, however, as he thought of himself as Acher, ascribing all his actions not to himself but to this 'other' person, he would not be able to begin the journey back.

We have to own up to who we are. We must not fake the story of our life, as an uneasy conscience often makes us do, repeating it over and over again in a vain effort to mitigate or dismiss those elements of it that most damage our self esteem. We have to face ourselves and face truth.

Maybe we feel: 'If once I dare admit that I've been wrong, there'll be no end of it. The whole of me is really rotten through.' But that is not the case. If we're not all good, we certainly aren't all bad. That is why it pains us so much to admit that we've been careless, thoughtless and cruel.

It is precisely because we are morally alive that our admissions hurt and sting. Only the inert conscience feels no shame. As pain is to the body, so shame may be to the soul. It may be the response of what is healthy when it encounters what is not. In these circumstances we can trust that painful sensation. Just as we have to live with our physical frailty, so must we acknowledge our moral vulnerability.

What is the alternative? It is that we blame all ills on others, spending our whole life frustrated by their undeniable faults while we remain totally and perfectly. That is the path of hatred. One day, if we follow that path, a really ugly 'other' will ambush and devour us.

Albrecht Goes, a pastor in the German Protestant Church who has devoted a large portion of his life's work to Christian Jewish reconciliation, once said: 'I believe we have learned all over again what the countenance of a man who is truly able to help men looks like. It is a face from which stubbornness, cocksureness, the worshipping of success, rigidity, and a pedantic clinging to principles increasingly vanish to give way to other, greater, realities: astonishment, the ability to be frightened, defencelessness, reverence, awe, gratitude.'[2] It is easy to understand why Goes refers to reverence and awe as characteristic of such a person, but why does he include defencelessness and the ability to be frightened? Perhaps the answer is that vulnerability, the capacity to recognise oneself as susceptible to weakness and error, is not just the window through which we let truth, but also the door through which we let others and their sufferings and needs, into our life.

Unless we are honest with ourselves we will not be fair to other people. If we hide from ourselves we shall have to hide from them as well. No wonder, then, that the first words we must take with us on the journey to meet God are those of acknowledgement and truth.

1 Rebbe Nachman of Breslav in *Sefer HaMiddot,* Agudat Meshech HaNachal, Jerusalem 5746, page 121.

2 Albrecht Goes in 'Go, Suffer, Wait: Three Gifts from Israel', an address given in Hamburg on 11 March 1962, in *Men of Dialogue*, Martin Buber and Albrecht Goes, edited by W. Rollins and H. Zohn, Funk and Wagnal, New York, 1969, page 270.

6 Forgive us, for we have sinned; pardon us, for we have done wrong

THE CONFESSION PRAYERS

To seek atonement is to be conscious of two things. On the one hand there is the recognition that we have done wrong, on the other the trust that forgiveness may be possible. The former awareness has to come from within ourselves; for the latter quality, so our tradition teaches us, we depend on God. We shall not however discover it there if we cannot at the same time find it in ourselves; in seeking forgiveness we must seek to be forgiving.

These matters are not easy. 'Forgiven and forgotten', one says. Without such readiness to make up our petty squabbles life, except for the hermit, would be impossible. Only the mean spirited hang on grimly to the memory of every offence committed against them. Nevertheless in the bigger issues 'forgiven and forgotten' does not take us very far. We cannot be released from serious responsibilities by the turn of an easy phrase. Of course, there are those who pardon themselves, and imagine they have pardoned others, all too easily. There are those, too, who are artificially forgiving, releasing the perpetrators from a guilt which they must face up to before their victims. For real forgiveness implies heart work, courage, the readiness to learn from life and to try to change our ways. Forgetfulness, on the contrary, is a kind of amnesia of the conscience; a person or a people that always forgets is morally unsound.

We have to remember; we must face the painful consciousness of what we have done wrong. That is not to say that we should feel permanently and inherently guilty. Judaism does not teach that people are wicked, that we do bad from birth. But it does require us to acknowledge that every one of us has the potential for doing wrong and giving hurt. Events, inevitably, test us and in the course of time we are exposed to just those situations that find our failings out. For each of us there is some situation that rings the inner bell, rousing the part that is the worst and just the very hardest to control.

It is profoundly disturbing to make contact with the ugliness inside. It spoils the image of the person we would like to think we are. It fills us with dismay, also anger at what provoked it into action. 'You made me feel like this! It's your fault, and the situation's fault and life's fault!' we say. For a while we may seek not atonement but revenge.

But then a different mood emerges and shame comes flooding through. For at heart I know that whatever the excuse, whatever the very real reasons, for there may well be causes outside myself, there is wrong within me too. I want to atone for it and put it right. I do not want to suffer the diminution of heart and soul which the harbouring of such emotions brings. I remember the love I have been given, the closeness of friends, the good things there have been, the beauty I have noticed. I do not want to be unworthy of all these. Therefore I seek to be clean again, knowable before God throughout my inner being. But can one trust in God's forgiveness? Wrong has turned to shame, but will it encounter understanding or rejection?

This question cannot be answered without reference to that ubiquitous word which is far more common in our liturgy than any condemnatory term: love. As, hopefully, children learn that their parents love them despite their naughtiness or nastiness, and that this love penetrates even the firm discipline of chastisement, so, we are taught, God's love is stronger than all else. Come near therefore, says God, be known. True, the intimation of that love may manifest itself in us in the feeling of remorse. But that in itself is a good thing, an acknowledgement of bad that depends on the recognition of good. It is a force, furthermore, for change. The danger is that we may have no faith in the love or in the shame. It is the children who dare not come near their parents, who either cannot trust or who have good reason not to trust that they are loved, who are truly deprived and morally at risk. God, our tradition teaches, the very real and human experience of those who have found God teaches, is not like that.

What then are the barriers to forgiveness and forgiving? They are not in God but in ourselves. Maybe we are too easy on ourselves, deluding ourselves into imagining we have let go of grudges we still harbour. Maybe we are too proud. Maybe we feel there is so little good inside us that if we ever admit to being wrong the bad within will swallow it all up. Maybe we feel there is so little good around us that if we tell our faults we'll be ridiculed and shamed.

But out of our own predicament we can understand the difficulties of others. They too need to know that they will be met with understanding; they too fear that their faults will be rubbed in. Can we, therefore, take a step back from our own feelings and try to comprehend them? We know too well the defensive harshness with which we shield our conscience's vulnerable flanks. Can we give others safe passage to the refuge of honest understanding and a fair hearing?

We are enjoined to forgive those who may have wronged us, but we are not required to be dishonest about what we think has happened. It would be mistaken to ignore our own perception of reality and fake a forced and insincere conciliation. In the long run we will only resent it more. We must remain true to ourselves. But part of that truth is the awareness of our own desire to be forgiven. It is the same love and understanding that we seek, the same God to whom we turn, the same longing to be innocent and whole that drives us and others to seek conciliation. Neither sins nor grudges are easily shed; we have to work on both.

7 Let our affliction ascend from evening, Let our forgiveness come from morning

THE KOL NIDREI SERVICE

On this night we, like our ancestor Jacob, wrestle with our angel. Even though it leave us limping, we must not let it go until it blesses us.

Jacob's story is familiar enough. Returning home after twenty years of exile, he fears the impending encounter with his brother Esau. During the night he therefore fords the river Yabok which marks the border with his mother country and divides his household into two camps for greater safety. Then he remains alone. A 'man' appears from nowhere and fights with him till dawn. 'Let me go', the mysterious figure demands, but Jacob refuses till he blesses him. Afterwards Jacob calls the place 'Peni'el', saying that he has seen God face to face.

On the night of Kol Nidrei we too are alone. Of course we meet together in congregations; the sense of community is one of the beauties of the day. We even confess in the plural, accepting our share of responsibility for the wrongs of society as a whole. But in our deeper reflections we inevitably remain apart. For it is our own life we must reflect on, my mortality, my decisions, my mistakes and my betrayals. In this knowledge, with this responsibility, we stand alone before the all-comprehending God of truth, from whom there is no escape.

At such a moment there appears the figure with whom we too must struggle. Who is it? Who was the unnamed stranger who came to Jacob from nowhere? To our Rabbis he was the guardian angel of Esau, exacting payment at this opportune time for wrongs committed long since. But he is something else as well. For we must bear in mind that it is twenty years since, fleeing home, Jacob passed this way. Returning to so significant a place, recalling in himself the younger man who dreamt here his great dream, there pass through Jacob's mind all chances and adventures that have fallen to him since. That night Jacob struggles with the person he has become.

Who have we become in the last year, or ten, or twenty? What have we done or said that haunts us, and what that satisfies our soul? What memories oppress us, what recollections give us joy? And what have we managed, long ago, to forget? There is no time like the night time for opening the narrow passage by which the painful, and the joyous, realisations rise up from the depths of the heart and force themselves upon the mind.

What also of the person we have not become? What have we not done or said that we might have done or said? It is related that at a funeral once the rabbi could not coax the weeping husband to return from the fresh-filled grave of his wife:

'It's time to go back now,' said the rabbi.

'Oh, no!' said the husband, 'you don't understand.'

'It's time to go back,' the well meaning minister said again.

'Oh, no, rabbi, you can't possibly understand. I loved my wife!'

'Indeed! Inevitably, however . . . '

'I loved her, and once I even almost told her so.'

As haunting as the memory of what we've done is the vivid recollection of what we've failed to do or say.

How, finally, do we come to terms with all the things we have not done and not deserved but that life has done to us? For life, being far from fair, grants joys unequally and unevenly exacts pain. Perhaps the greatest of all our struggles is this: to forgive life; to let go where we must lose; to be reconciled to the death of one whose company was the substance, most often the joy of all our days; to accept our separations and our limitations; to release the stopper and empty out the vial of bitterness that, after all, would poison only us; to be grateful for who we are and what we have.

With all these things we wrestle till the rising of the dawn. What then? Do we finally let the vexing apparitions go and weary and defeated welcome rest, as, after a bad night, the insomniac at last drifts off to sleep five minutes before the alarm?

Surely not! Like Jacob, we shall not set our memories free until our very battle brings us blessing. Some of our greatest, our most worthwhile victories are those we win within ourselves. The gains may not be very showy, but they are real: understanding, the capacity to forgive both self and others, and compassion. These are the blessings that come with dawn. They, after our long battle with ourselves, are the dawn.

'And Jacob called the name of the place Peniel: "for I have seen God face to face, and my life has been preserved".' (Bereshit 32: 31). Here, as great truth, seemingly an invasion, wells up from within us and explores us and accuses and consoles us, we have our meeting with God. Not in heaven but in our conscience and our soul do we see God face to face.

1 Rabbi Jack Riemer in *The World of the Holy Days*, Bernie Books, Miami, Florida, 1991.

8 As we remember on this sacred day our revered and beloved kinsfolk who have gone to their eternal rest . . .

THE YIZKOR SERVICE

We know well enough what separates us from the past: time and death. But what unites us with it? What, if any, are the bonds that transcend our mortal nature?

This question came into my mind with great force as I stood in a park in Scotland watching my little boy play. I grew up in Scotland and my childhood felt as close as touch. Perhaps my parents or my grandparents took me to this place, by this stream, in these mountains? Did one love not extend from them to the child that used to play and thence to the child now playing? The feeling was so immediate that I felt my mother standing with me. At once a sense of separation cut the bond and there I was alone and unprotected. After all, one can't expect the hills and rivers to care. Our transient passage is an irrelevance to the world around us. When we are gone our place 'shall know us no more' (Job 7: 10).

Is there anything that death cannot annul?

During the last year there have been a number of programmes about children who survived the holocaust in hiding. One of them contained an interview with a man in his late fifties now living on a kibbutz He had grown up in Budapest. In 1944, when he was a very little boy, he and his mother were herded with many others down to the Danube. Realising that what awaited them was certain death, she handed him to a total stranger. He became a street child, living in dustbins. But he survived and went to Israel where he married and had children of his own. He had asked himself many times, he observed at the end of the interview, how, after all he had been through, he was able to live a normal life free from bitterness. I can only think, he said, that the great love my mother gave me has been with me ever since.

In another programme they interviewed a woman who said that after the war was over she had lived through other terrors. For through all those crucial years of childhood there had been no one to teach her how to love.

The love we are given and the love we give are not destroyed by death. Only we have the power to destroy them. How great is our responsibility, then, to unpick the crust of cynicism that so readily seals the adult heart, to be kind, generous and warm and to eschew cruelty and hate. Perhaps when this task seems hard we too need to remember the hidden child that lives in each of us, and its need to be taught to love.

Love is strong; love expressed in the context of a shared tradition is even stronger. Thus the path of Jewish life and practice binds the generations together in the companionship of common history and faith. We remember what our grandparents or parents did on Rosh Hashanah and Yom Kippur, the tunes they used at the Seder table, the Synagogues to which they brought us. Small things ('he loved this melody') recall great attachments. But over and above our individual memories and affections, our prayers and our observances unite us with our ancestors as a whole. They enable us to form one living chain of spirit with them, back to Joseph Caro, to Maimonides and Rabbi Akiva and Moses. We seek God along the same path down which their spirits are our guides. Following thus the way of the commandments, which they have helped define for us, we find a warmth and wisdom which words may perhaps describe to us but only experience can transmit. We share our search for God and in so doing find each other in a world of spiritual meanings which death cannot erode. Our Torah is indeed a tree of everlasting life.

Yet there remains something still greater through which we transcend the limitations of death. For though love binds us to our personal and tradition to our communal past, the presence of God, encompassing all things, unites with all beings that have ever lived or ever will. 'In Thy hand are the souls of the living and the dead,' we pray. So we deeply hope, though naturally we fear that we will be extinguished at our death, that we will slip inexorably over the precipice of life and down to annihilation. Yet the seekers of God and poets and people of all nations have intuited a presence which embraces all that is and was and will be, including it in one invincible life:

And I have felt
A presence that disturbs me with the joy
Of elevated thoughts; a sense sublime
Of something far more deeply interfused,
Whose dwelling is the light of setting suns,
And the round ocean, and the living air,
And the blue sky, and in the mind of man,
A motion and a spirit, that impels
All thinking things, all objects of all thought,
And rolls through all things.[1]

We will all die, but our work of heart and spirit will find homes in heart and spirit.

1 William Wordsworth: Lines written a few miles above Tintern Abbey.

9 Open unto us the gates at the time of the closing of the gates

THE NEILAH SERVICE

Rabbi Yochanan holds that the gates locked at Ne'ilah are the Temple gates; Rav considers them to be the gates of heaven, now shutting with the dark. The most relevant gates, however, are not outside us but within. Never mind the closing, the urgency of the hour calls us anew to the hard task of opening them up. If we have not yet done so over these days, can we now at this weary but exalted time draw them open into ourselves. 'We live only once. Do we not want to live fully? The corridor of life stretches before us . . . This then is the meaning of Ne'ilah, the call to the doors which we never opened.'[1]

Inner gates are the hardest of all to open. There are many rooms inside which we would far rather keep closed. Virtually every life is marked by matters that are too painful to bear thinking on; we shield them from our scrutiny. The opening of a door permits bright light to flow over many hidden things. Nevertheless at this Ne'ilah service we must try to open gates. Which ones should they be?

First let us open the gate of truth. The first truth that we have to live with is that this is no rehearsal; it's for real. It is our life, to all practical intents and purposes our one and only opportunity here on earth. Yet, obvious as it is, this is a fact with which it is difficult to live. Our origin is in dust and our earthly end is our return to dust. At the risk of our life we earn our bread. We are like clay that shatters, grass that withers, flowers that fade, a dream that flies away. What, then, are we doing with our time, with this brief life that is ours nonetheless to shape?

Next let us open the gates of shame. Shame is not the same as public humiliation or disgrace. Shame can be the quiet inner teacher of our moral being. It is as if we were to spread a blackout curtain around our rib cage and watch from within the film of our life play itself back in our heart. We would be given, before we viewed it, a sensitivity and conscience we may often have lacked at the time. How hard it would be to watch! We would say to ourselves: How many important things I ignored! Of how much beauty, of how much suffering was I heedless! How many people did I wrong! Perhaps, after all, it would be better not to see the film? And yet I want to know and before God I want to be known. In the paradoxical privacy of our communal confessions I want to see myself more truly and learn from what I find. God, after all, knows already; I can't seek God and lie about myself.

Open in us next the gates of understanding and of wisdom. Fear and envy often close those doors. Remove from us the need always to be right, to be unassailable. Let us discover, as Ben Zoma taught, how to learn from all people.[2] In his famous discourse about them Job asks the question: 'Whence does wisdom come and what is the place of understanding?' [28: 20]. This is the plain meaning of the verse, but it is possible to read the Hebrew word for 'whence' – 'Me'ayyin' – differently, for 'Me'ayyin' can also mean 'from nowhere'. Understanding, the verse would then say, comes from nowhere, from being as nothing, from the readiness to listen to life without prejudice or pride.

Open in us the gates of gratitude and appreciation. How much of our life do we really notice and how much slips by without our recognition? If we were to be shown that film of our own life including all we'd ever done, many of us would spend our time exclaiming: 'Was I really there? I never noticed at the time!' In spite of, perhaps because of, all we do, we are often absent from our own and only life. In fact, the sheer volume of our activities may be a measure of our very lack of heed, and our many and constant needs an index to how little we actually value or find sustaining in our lives. Don't, God, let us miss our life. Let us notice more, and care.

For in the end our capacity for gratitude will be the measure of us all. Otherwise we will always be dissatisfied and unable to make good use of what the world has offered us. Without a sense of gratitude we will find it even harder, when the time comes, to cede life with good grace. This is perhaps the hardest challenge, especially today, for, as Rabindranath Tagore has written: 'We are not trained to recognise the inevitable as natural, and so cannot give up gracefully that which has to go, but needs must wait till it is snatched from us. The truth comes as conqueror only because we have lost the art of receiving it as guest.'[3] Therefore open in us the gates of acceptance.

Then finally open the gates of love. Make our hearts tractable to its power. Open us to that love which has a clear, tangible object; the love of family, friends, the stranger, animals, plants. And open us also to the love which has no especial object, to the love which comes from and returns to You, passing on its way through all things, the very life of all creation. For it is to this that we ultimately dedicate our lives, saying twice daily that we shall try to love the Lord our God with all our heart and all our soul and all our might.

1 Milton Steinberg in *Yearnings*, The Rabbinical Assembly, New York, 1968, page 29.

2 Ben Zoma in Pirkei Avot, the Chapters of the Fathers, 4: 1.

3 Rabindranath Tagore, 'The Four Stages of Life', in *The World Treasury of Modern Religious Thought*, edited by Jaroslav Pelikan, Little, Brown and Company, 1990, page 153.

10 And you shall rejoice before the Lord your God

LEVITICUS 23: 40

Succot is the festival of fulfilment, the season of our joy, the celebration of innocence restored. It is the time when we leave our homes and, sitting beneath the leaves which symbolise God's protective presence, appreciate with a wanderer's gratitude the fruits and colours of the autumn.

I always look forwards to the moment when after returning from the Synagogue at the end of Yom Kippur I can take the hammer and bang in the first nail of the Succah. If the long fast has gone badly a nail is a very safe thing to hit out at. If it's gone well and the day has taken us to the heights, then here is a marvellously practical way of coming back down to earth.

Succot does indeed bring us down to earth in a spirit of childlike joy. If Yom Kippur involves the affliction of the senses then Succot requires us to appreciate the pleasure that they bring. On no other festival do we speak so much of 'hiddur mitzvah', fulfilling the mitzvot beautifully, or of 'noi', adornment – in this case of the Succah. On Succot each of our senses must rejoice.

For the eye there is the booth itself. Technically speaking the walls may of course be left bare, though the roof must be made of greenery. But such a minimalist attitude has never been the Jewish way. All around is the foliage of early autumn to cut and prune from with its yellows, orange, red and late deep greens. There are rose hips, apples and many garden fruits. The entire Succah can be a celebration of these natural glories while from the roof hang fruits, carrots, radishes, anything bright, and a pumpkin well tied on.

For the ear there is the sound of the wind through branches (not too strong a wind, one hopes, lest the Succah, which to be legal must withstand an average gust, be demolished by a gale). Then there is the singing, the Kiddush and the grace after meals drifting across the gardens, making non-Jewish neighbours wonder yet again at the strange (but charming) customs these Jewish people have.

Scents were permitted on Yom Kippur; smell being considered the most spiritual of the senses its pleasures were not forbidden. But what did they amount to? 'Halitosis', as one congregant put it, 'and the reviving reek of ammonia when someone thrusts a bottle of salts beneath your nose'. But on Succot there is the fragrance of fruit and flowers, the cold vitality of early morning mist, and chief among all, the scent of the Etrog. I once saw a dying man take an Etrog and, in breathing in the smell, inhale all the memories of his childhood of which he then began to speak. He kept it by his bedside till the end.

For touch there is the feel of the sharp Lulav; also, on a wet night in the Succah, the steady drip of rain down the back of one's neck.

What can one say about taste? Everyone has their Succot favourite. One of my earliest memories is of my mother throwing a handful of sweets for us to gather in the Succah. But on the whole the dishes for this festival have the common quality, at least in northern lands, of conserving heat: thick soups, baked potatoes and stuffed cabbage rolls. For every meal must be eaten in the Succah and the pious are not put off by bad weather.

Succot is the celebration of life. But it is an unpossessive joy we share. We find it not in what we have and hold, in our solid homes, but out beneath the sky under what the mystics called the canopy of faith. For it is good to appreciate the world we are privileged to live in, right to be grateful for the gifts that it can bring.

Rosh Hashanah and Yom Kippur remind us of our mortality. They bring home to us our weaknesses both physical and moral. But in so doing they restore to us the capacity to value, while we share them, the gifts of time and world. On Succot we should enjoy them, with fresh heart and innocent touch.

The Simple Guide To Succah Building

1 A Succah needs three walls. (You can get away with two and a bit but the rules are complicated, so stick to three.) A fourth wall will give more protection, but isn't halachically required.

2 The walls may be made of anything. Existing walls may be used. (e.g. A Succah can be made where the garden fence and house wall meet, where only one additional wall would be required.)

3 The structure needn't be perfect. It has to be able to withstand an average inland wind.

4 The walls must be at least ten handbreadths high; forty inches is generally considered sufficient. (But you may want to be able to stand up in the Succah, so as long as you don't exceed the upper limit of thirty feet, you will probably want to build higher.)

5 The floor area of the Succah must be at least seven handbreadths by seven handbreadths, or two foot six by two foot six. But, as it is a Mitzvah to entertain guests in the Succah, you may prefer something a little bigger.

6 The roof is what makes the Succah a Succah. It must be specially made for the festival. Two rules govern the substances (Sechach) to be used: They must grow from the ground (but be severed from the point of growth – e.g. cut branches). They must not be capable of becoming ritually impure. To be safe, use branches (but not ones with poisonous berries or leaves which immediately wilt) or matting bought as Sechach.

7 The branches on the roof should be thick enough for the shaded area to be greater than the sunlit area on the succah floor. They should not be so thick that the stars cannot be seen through them.

8 The branches may be supported on bamboos, netting or thin trellis, but the branches must provide the majority of the covering.

9 It is a Mitzvah to make the Succah a place of beauty. To this end, flowers, fruits and vegetables, as well as drawings and coloured fabrics should be used to decorate the walls.

10 A Succah may be built in a garden, a courtyard, on a balcony, a ship, a cart or the back of a camel (though the latter is not advised as one is forbidden to enter it on Yom Tov). In certain circumstances a conservatory roof may be lifted and replaced with Sechach, but halachic advice will be required.

Much joy – little effort – Have a go!
Chag Sameach!

The editor would like to thank:

Rabbi Dr Louis Jacobs and Jewish Chronicle Publications, London, for permission to reprint the numerous extracts from Rabbi Louis Jacobs *A Guide to Rosh Hashanah* (second impression, 1962) and *A Guide to Yom Kippur* (third impression, 1966).

Rabbi Jack Riemer for permission to reprint numerous extracts by him from *The World of the High Holy Days,* vols. I and II, edited by Rabbi J. Riemer, Bernie Books, Miami 1991 and 1992

The Rabbinical Assembly, New York, for permission to reprint: 'Prelude to the Avodah Service' in Sh. Ansky: 'The Dybbuk', adapted by Rabbi Jules Harlow from Bialik's translation; and 'Neilah' by Rabbi Milton Steinberg, both from *Yearnings*, 1968.

The Prayer Book Press of Media Judaica, Bridgeport, Connecticut 06605, USA for permission to reprint 'All Vows' by Harold Kushner from page 402 of Mahzor Hadash, the New Mahzor, edited by Rabbi Sidney Greenberg and Rabbi Jonathan D. Levine, (*c.*1978).

The Reform Synagogues of Great Britain, London, for permission to reprint the comment by Rabbi Zusya of Hanipol from *Forms of Prayer for Jewish Worship; volume III, Prayers for High Holydays,* page 6 (1985).

Vera Gissing and Robson Books Ltd. London, for permission to reprint the letter from her mother in *Pearls of Childhood,* paperback edition, 1994 page 154–5.

Ina Hughs for permission to reprint 'A Prayer For Children'. Ina Hughs is author of *A Prayer for Children,* William Morrow and Company Inc., New York, 1995.

Rabbi Arnold Turetsky, for permission to reprint 'A Story Before We Begin' from *The World of the High Holy Days,* volume I, page 71, edited by Rabbi J. Riemer, Bernie Books, Miami, 1991.

Rabbi David Wolpe for permission to reprint 'Why do we Confess our Sins we have not Done? from *The World of the High Holy Days,* volume II, page 275, edited by Rabbi J. Riemer, Bernie Books, Miami, 1992.

It was not possible to trace James Kavanaugh whose poem 'Once I Believed' is reprinted with gratitude to the author.

The Hebrew Calligraphy is by Vetta Alexis, London.

The picture of the lamp is by Barbara Jackson, London.

The Assembly of Masorti Synagogues works for reasonableness and responsiblity within tradition.

Typeset by Antony Gray; printed and bound in Great Britain by Antony Rowe Ltd, Chippenham, Wiltshire.